CREATIVE

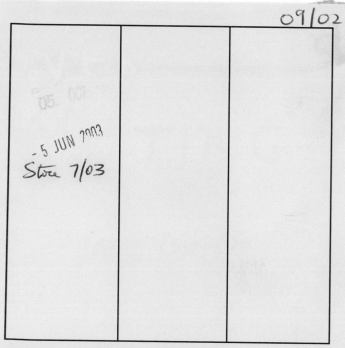

A & C Black • London

500 758 319

First published in 2002 by
A & C Black Publishers Limited
37 Soho Square, London W1D 3QZ
www.acblack.com

© 2002 Jane Dorner

ISBN 0 7136 5854 1

A CIP catalogue record for this book is available from the British Library.

Jane Dorner is identified as the author of this book in accordance with Chapter 77 of the Copyright, Designs and Patents Act, 1988.

The author and the publishers have done their best to ensure the accuracy of all information in this book. They can accept no responsibility for content found as a result of following links in the book.

A & C Black uses paper produced with elemental chlorine-free pulp, harvested from managed sustainable forests.

Typeset in 10.5 on 12pt Janson

Printed and bound in Great Britain by
Creative Print and Design (Wales), Ebbw Vale

Contents

Foreword

by Terry Pratchett

The thing to remember about Picasso, someone once said, was that although he might paint your mum blue and square, if you held a gun to his head he was capable of proper art.

So read on...

The web needs this book, heaven knows, and Jane got the hang of word-processing while the rest of us were still sticking old Scrabble letters to the paper with glue.

There's so much happening out there, some of which is breathtaking, a lot of which is intriguing, some of which is amusing and occasional bits of which make me wish I had that gun. This book is your guide. In a sense, it's a map of an avalanche. Tomorrow will be different. But I was incredibly pleased to read that things stay the same, because we are all human, (except maybe for a few people in the Bay area). However pretty the pixels, this is still largely a text-based medium. There are rules. Grammar, spelling and punctuation need to enter your life, if only for a brief holiday. You need to understand what a narrative is. You need to understand what a contract is, too, because although the web is wild and free, lawyers are expensive. You have to grasp that you can't break the rules properly without knowing what the rules are, and that it's useful to understand geography if you're trying to break new ground.

And you need to hone these skills because the really interesting stuff hasn't been done yet. Remember: the first modern aeroplane was flown by two men who were good at building bicycles.

Terry Pratchett

Acknowledgements

The books and online texts that I have read and been influenced by are listed on page 161. Where I have quoted directly, I have acknowledged that source within the text. However, thoughts and phrases are so easily transported in electronic formats that I may sometimes inadvertently have used a form of expression or sequence of examples without crediting the first owner. If that has happened, I apologise in advance and will put it right in any subsequent editions. As everyone knows, ideas come from many different sources and each individual adds their personal spin. And who can be totally pure in a world where electronic note-taking catches in the clipboards? To quote my favourite three aperçus:

> 'If you steal from one author, it's plagiarism; if you steal from many, it's research.' (Wilson Mizner)

> 'If you copy from three sources, it is scientific work.' (unknown)

> 'A good composer does not imitate, he steals.' (Stravinsky)

The e-text from which the Aladdin story is quoted comes from the Project Gutenberg archives.

My thanks to Mary Cavil, Jess Curtis and Susanna Gladwin for reading and commenting on the drafts of this book; to Diane Greco for permission to quote from her interview in 'Eastgate Now' on page 99; to Carolyn Guertin for letting me eavesdrop on her online writing course, 'Textual Machines: Building Web-based Narratives'; to Edward Picot for sharing an (at-the-time) unpublished essay on 'Reading Sideways' with me; to Sue Thomas for many interesting conversations; to Alexis Weedon for setting up a survey on electronic reading for me with her students; to Tim Wright for permission to adapt a section from his presentation at the Riverside Studios in September 2001; and to Hazel Bell for the Index and for passing interesting snippets from her reading to me.

All the artists quoted have given me their permission.

The Kurt Schwitters poem *An Anna Blume* on pp. 82–3 is reproduced by kind permission of DuMont Literatur und Kunst Verlag GmbH & Co.

Preface

When Bill Clinton became President of the United States in 1993, there were 50 websites. When he stood down in 2001 there were 350 million. In the second Christmas of his presidency *The Guardian* carried a short item reporting that the White House had – innovatively – put its card on the web. The article coupled my name with that of Bill and Hillary for doing the same thing, mentioning my 'winter solstice intertextual greeting' which, like the Clintons' card, was on the web. This was at a time when the only options were black print with blue links on grey screens – unappealing and unattractive, but *The Guardian* wondered if this would be how everyone would send their Christmas greetings in the future.

I had shamelessly adapted a Shakespeare sonnet into 14 lines about the endurance of words on screens (a spoof version of rhyme outliving brass, stone and the gilded monuments of princes), and I popped in some rather trivial hyperlinks and a picture or two. I suppose that was my first piece of creative web writing and I saw it as a comment on the cultural icons of the time.

I have been commenting on – and experimenting with – the culture of the web ever since. I have not yet made up my mind whether the web will revolutionise creative writing or whether it is simply an extension of what we have had before, the difference being that the web offers more people more chance of making an impact. And I have not made up my mind whether the chaos, anarchy, chatter and noise of the web obscure its possibilities as a means of communicating serious, reflective literature. The web celebrates a fusion of image, word and disconcerting animation; it enjoys fragmentary and provocative phrases, quirky typesetting, dazzling effects and disparate leaps of thought. The literature I most value tells me something about the human condition in language I can appreciate and understand, and language seems to be the most unambiguous way of conveying the insights that we hunger after. At the same time, the logical, reasoning route to meaning is not the only one: sometimes being open to imaginative experience is more powerful. Perhaps computers and technology seem unlikely vehicles for inspiration, but let's be open to what they can offer. The unpredictability of web spaces has a certain verve and freshness that challenges an observer's passivity.

There are tensions here that this book cannot but reflect. The web is as yet too young a medium, and I am as suspicious of it as I am admiring. What I present in this book, then, are the opportunities that I have found for writers and for students of writing; those reading it must make up their own minds what value those opportunities offer to them individually. It is only by *doing* that one truly realises the artistic potential of a medium. I have experimented with the breadth of possibilities, but not the depth – it is up to those who follow the leads in this book to do that.

Navigation note

This book addresses different kinds of writers as well as teachers of writing. I make no apology for that – web writing is inclusive and overlapping. It is also an unfamiliar term and one to which different readers will attach different meanings. The Introduction shows that web writing is not writing about the web, nor is it writing code for web pages (though that may come into it); and the book is structured as follows.

Part 1 explores the web as a superb advertising and delivery showcase for printed works of all kinds. There are whole sets of new publishers cashing in on this, as well as individual authors who bypass publishers altogether. The variety of formats and delivery mechanisms are mostly dealt with in Chapter 1, page 24. This isn't 'creative web writing'; it is using the web to *supply* creative writing.

Part 2 looks at the web as a medium for new forms of creativity (though having its roots in the past); one that involves experimentation with writing and pushing out its boundaries as a linear form. Chapter 3 shows some ways in which artists are doing this. However, you will not find any post-modernist theory in these pages: it seems to me that it is for the artist to experiment with new forms, and for the critics to come along afterwards with a set of labels if they so desire.

Part 2 includes some illustrations of creative web writing that must be seen on the web to gain full impact. The quotations given to illustrate a point are out-of-context and will rarely give the flavour of the experience. I have given the URLs as they were in mid 2002; Internet addresses change, however, and when the next round of top-level domain names are announced some of the URLs will alter. Most are likely to have redirections on them, but some will not. In such a case, readers should go to the Google search engine[1] and type in the proper names of anything mentioned in this book. If it still exists, Google will find it.

[1] <http://www.google.com/>

Part 3 is the practical section, commenting on stylistic points and providing listings that are the result of many hours of research and assessment. They cannot be exhaustive, but should provide the web writer with ideas and starting points to stimulate new ideas and lead to new markets. Many of the sites mentioned here will also be added to the website of my previous book, *The Internet: A Writer's Guide* (2nd Edition 2001)[2], and technical details about the Internet explained in that book will not be repeated here.

Readers may wish to zig-zag between the various parts – for example, issues about screen readability apply whether you are writing conventionally or innovatively. My own view is that the iconoclasts will come back to value readability – but time will tell.

[2] <http://www.internetwriter.co.uk/>

Introduction

The magician said: 'Fear nothing, but obey me. Beneath this stone lies a treasure which is to be yours, and no one else may touch it, so you must do exactly as I tell you.' At the word treasure Aladdin forgot his fears, and grasped the ring as he was told.

This book is about a new medium that offers new creative opportunities. It is not about writing or designing *for* websites; rather, it is about how the existence of the web can augment or change literary genres or add a new range of hues to the already rich writing palette. It is about how creative writing exists within a continuum from the past, and how experimentation ploughs back into traditional writing forms.

At a functional level, the very existence of the Internet (the overarching system connecting all websites) makes it easier for writers to find an audience. At a creative level, it offers rewards to the brave. If you want to be one of the brave, read on. If you want to wait until the medium has settled, watch others make mistakes and lose time or money, and only join in when conventions and technical constraints have settled, then read on too. New art forms need both the brave and the cautious.

Let's remember that the book is a technology which took centuries to perfect in the form we know it now. Even something as obvious as spaces between words did not become standard in the West until the seventh century – beautiful as early bibles were, accessibility was restricted to the privileged. Even after the invention of print in 1455, it took more than 50 years to establish conventions such as page numbering, paragraphing, legible typefaces, title pages, chapter divisions, indexes, footnotes and all the parts that make the book so easy to read and navigate. Books printed before 1501 are called *incunabula*, which comes from the Latin meaning 'swaddling clothes' and seems to indicate that these works came from a technology still in its infancy. Fictional and non-fictional forms developed, in a leisurely manner, with the evolution of the coherent product that the book became. I will argue that much of the work on the web at present is in infant form, and, like the young, gazes inwards, obsessed by itself. Web writing has some growing up to do before it can reach out beyond the first limping steps it is taking at present.

In terms of development, film narrative and documentary were a little faster off the mark than books. It took around a century for these to mature to their highly sophisticated present state. One of the first examples of technical cinematography was the Louis Le Prince film of Leeds bridge in 1888, and arguably the first creative use was when Edwin Porter demonstrated the power of editing in *Life of an American Fireman* in 1902. Porter was the first to show what was possible by manipulating the relationship of successive shots. There is little agreement on what one judges as the start of creative film-making: what we can say, however, is that it didn't attract the Edwardian writers of the day as a story-telling genre. Perhaps writers like H G Wells, John Galsworthy and Arnold Bennett might have seen film as a vehicle for their ideas if they had been able to jump on Wells's own time machine to a future in which screen-writing was lucrative and prestigious.

In like manner, web writing does not attract the well-known writers of our day. There are many reasons for this, which this book will explore further. Fame and fortune undoubtedly figure, so that in general, only people with capital, a day job associated with Internet culture, or with time on their hands are able to explore the web's contribution to innovative story-telling. We're at the 'flicker' stage, just as we were when we called early cinema 'the flicks' because it was so primitive and unstable. Progress towards a popular new art-form will be exponentially faster. However, the web has been with us for a mere handful of years and its potential as a recreational medium is still being tested. 1990 marked its 'official' beginning, but only towards the end of that decade was it cheap enough, and of sufficiently friendly design, to extend into the home.

Websites still appear tangled by contrast to the coherence of books and films. Sometimes you feel as if you are turning pieces of a Rubik cube, seeking to match all nine squares of colour on a single face of the cube and yet always ending up with non-matching squares. We haven't yet established conventions of segmentation and navigation. The separation of the printed book into discrete chapters allowed the modern novel to develop; hypertext fiction is still waiting for developments like this to take it into the next phase.

My own theory, which I hope to develop in the course of this book, is that everything that is currently occurring on the web is a development of events in literature so far. In some cases it is a step backwards, because some of the hard-learned truths about the way people read and what they appear to want from imaginative writing have been thrown out of the window to make way for anarchic innovation. Even this anarchy is nothing new, although it may well be that the experimental phase we are in now is forcing writers who are playing with the web to step several paces back – *reculer pour mieux sauter.*

Although the web has all the resources of audio, video and animation at its disposal, sound and moving pictures don't squeeze easily down ordinary people's telephone wires or cabling. You need broadband for that (think of broadband as a number of lanes on a motorway, allowing more cars to travel at a reasonable speed rather than being snagged up in a traffic jam). So the narrative opportunities are still well before the 'talkies' in filmic terms. That is because technical resourcing makes the web essentially text-based.

It is inevitable that whatever we produce on the web now will look quaint in some years' time. But in the meantime, there is a real opportunity for writers to make their mark and to influence the way in which narrative on the web develops. You could say that writers are poised to win or lose this particular piece of the creative terrain *now*. If we don't seize the initiative, then the games designers, programmers, animators and technicians will dictate what happens next.

A few far-sighted artistic people *are* experimenting and trying to find new entertainment paradigms. But no-one of genius has yet made the connections that will jump-start the web's randomness of hypertext linking into an absorbing experience. No Shakespeares or Blakes have shown others the way. Entertainment – at whatever artistic level – depends on bringing stories or situations to life. Where the web scores, is in the fact that those stories can be visual, musical and filmic. More than that, they can involve the recipient in ways which change the outcomes. No medium has yet done this effectively.

Web stories may be cybersoaps; they may be interactive dramas or personal diaries; they may be games; they may be in poetic form; they may be WAP-enabled phone-ins. But all will present an enormous challenge to the people writing and engineering them. Entertainment allowing for different outcomes according to the choices of the user requires very clever writing and programming, and our understanding of how this can be made successful is still at an early stage. If, as a society, we value creative people enough to support them through the experimental period, then we will be rewarded with a medium that *does* entertain us.

Writing motivation

Meanwhile, the web certainly attracts people who write. One of the fundamental issues about writing is why one has a need to write at all. For some people it is quite simply a necessity, a part of being a whole person. The question is not 'why do they write', but 'how could they possibly *not* write'? There's no single answer to that, and indeed, personal circumstances change. For example, I don't myself write poetry as a regular part of my life, but there have been times of extreme stress or confusion or heart-ache when prose just hasn't been able to express what I have wanted to say. On those occasions, I have turned to poetic forms. The poems I wrote at such times are very precious to me, because I still recognise what those feelings were and how minimalist language enabled me to pack dense thought into short lines. At the same time, though I have had some of them published, poetry is not my true milieu and I haven't worked at it, practised or become proficient in the language of poetry. I don't therefore expect other people to read my poems.

For some, however, any piece of writing requires an audience – even an audience of one – because what's important is not the writing itself, but the need for just one person to understand the thoughts, needs or meaning behind it. Others again – and here I do count myself – write for money: quite simply, writing is the way they have chosen to earn a living. The compass goes from hack journalism, advertising copy and functional explanations of all kinds through to screen-plays and literary fiction. If it didn't pay, the person doing it would have to turn to something else to earn a daily crust. Most members of the Society of Authors – all of whom are paid, practising writers – have to supplement their writing income with some other activity. A few celebrities at the tip of the iceberg earn real money and an even tinier 'tip' are rich.

For some, the motive force is vanity – the dubious pleasure of seeing one's name on screen. The old-fashioned term 'in print' is no longer applicable here, because in this book we are essentially talking about writing that is going to be read on a screen (rather than in conventional formats that use the web simply as a delivery mechanism). It's arguable that seeing your name on screen doesn't have quite the same lustre as running your fingers over the gilded lettering on a book jacket, and – if that is the case – then there is an immediate problem with the perception of onscreen or web writing.

Many writers reading this, however, will bridle at the notion that you can identify the complex reasons why people have a need to write, and why everything about writing in its many forms holds infinite fascination. Self-expression or money or fame may be what the writing brings, but they are not ends in themselves. Since there are many reasons for engaging in writing in the first place, it is also difficult to categorise kinds of writer – although in the print publishing world, that is exactly what does happen. To be saleable means to be genre-stamped as a romance writer, biographer, playwright, novelist, thriller writer, humorist, historian, journalist, translator, librettist, publicist, essayist – the list could extend to every category of the Dewey decimal system. What's new about the web is that these categorisations melt into each other. Because we no longer need to find a book in its correct place on a library shelf, or displayed appropriately in a bookshop, we no longer need to tag an individual as a particular kind of writer. Web writing offers fresh air because it cuts across boundaries we have so long accepted.

This is liberating, but it might also be uncomfortable, because however trite categorisations seem to be, it's human nature to try to see patterns – either in how individuals write, or in what forms the motive force for writing. Examples of two such attempts to categorise writing are given below, the first drawing on outer strategies and the second on inner ones – not because they are the only ones, but because each attempts to impose order on the disorder of writing. They are interesting for what each of us will recognise in ourselves, and relate to, as much as for the fact that all such categorisations offer a partial explanation of the motive force behind writing. Reflecting on them may enable individual writers to assess how their own strategies and psychology fit with the demands of the web.

Strategies

In *The Act of Writing*, academic Daniel Chandler[3] discusses writing techniques in the context of the prevailing technologies. Personal habits dictate how each of us approaches writing, and the technology of the day makes those strategies more or less successful. He identifies four common writing strategies which I will look at with web writing in mind.

[3] ISBN 0-903878-44-5, pp. 275, University of Wales, Aberystwyth, 1995

The architectural strategy

This involves conscious pre-planning and organisation, followed by writing out, with relatively limited revision. The metaphor of the writer as 'architect' is prominent in Neo-Classical literary theory, emphasising conscious planning and design. This is a distinct asset in web writing because without the ability to plan and structure, the resultant work could be random or aimless.

The bricklaying strategy

This involves polishing each sentence (or paragraph) before proceeding to the next. The completed text is not subjected to much subsequent revision. Chandler quotes an author who says: 'I have to get every paragraph as nearly right as possible before I go onto the next paragraph. I'm somewhat like a bricklayer: I build very slowly, not adding a new row until I feel that the foundation is solid enough to hold up the house. I'm the exact opposite of the writer who dashes off his entire first draft, not caring how sloppy it looks or how badly it's written.' If this is your tactic, my suspicion is that you will go on working in this manner, regardless of print or electronic reading.

The oil painting strategy

This involves minimal pre-planning and major revision. Ideas are jotted down as they occur and are organised later. The novelist Kurt Vonnegut reported: 'Usually I begin with several ideas, start playing with them. They are authentic concerns about things in life that bother me. One way of my dealing with them is in writing. I play with these ideas until they start to feel right. It's something like oil painting. You lay on paint and lay on paint. Suddenly you have something and you frame it.' The 'under-construction' nature of the web favours this; web writing need not ever be fixed, so the oil painter can go on adding layers ad lib.

The watercolour strategy

This involves producing a single version of a text relatively rapidly with minimal revision. Literary writers, it appears, often work in this way. For some writers it may be simply an initial strategy for producing a first draft; sometimes only for part of a text. John

Steinbeck worked this way because he felt that 'rewrite in process...
interferes with flow and rhythm which can only come from a kind
of unconscious association with the material'. Ray Bradbury similarly reported: 'I do a first draft as passionately and as quickly as I
can. I believe a story is only valid when it is immediate and pas-
sionate; when it dances out of your subconscious. If you interfere
with it in any way, you destroy it.' If it is indeed true that this is a
feature of literary writers' technique, then that tells us something
interesting about the web's failure to attract such writers. The technologies for bringing innovation into e-writing are cumbersome,
expensive and hard to learn. They are not intuitive and they probably get in the way of the watercolourist's brush-stroke.

Inner psychology

Writing strategy, of course, develops from one's inner psychology,
which gives some of the motive force behind why people write. In
The Forest for the Trees: An Editor's Advice to Writers, the experienced
editor Betsy Lerner[4] identifies five 'writer types', all of them familiar. Perhaps they give a clue to the qualities that a writer might
need to succeed in this environment.

The ambivalent writer

This is a writer who can't commit to one idea for a story from the
many possibles, and who does not realise that writing is 90 per cent
sheer sticking power. If procrastination is forever confused with
research, then perhaps the writer doesn't really need to write and
indeed shouldn't. After all, says Virginia Woolf, the world 'does not
care whether Flaubert finds the right word or whether Carlyle
scrupulously verifies this or that fact. Naturally, it will not pay for
what it doesn't want'. Ambivalence won't be missed. Curiously, the
web favours an element of dabbling in multiplicity, because hypertext allows for a certain amount of bouncing off at a tangent. As
long as the writer finds a way of structuring many ideas that are
satisfying for the reader, this can work. Ultimately, however,
ambivalence and lack of commitment will confuse readers and leave
them foundering. Readers still want to hand themselves into the
care of an all-knowing story-teller with a point of view.

[4] ISBN 1-57322-152-X, pp. 285, New York: Riverhead Books/Penguin Putnam, 2000

The natural writer

This is one for whom writing appears to come easily – or is that the myth of not realising that hard writing makes easy reading? Lerner's definition of the 'natural' is 'one who is always writing'. She cites Thurber, who never quite knew when he was or wasn't at it: 'Sometimes my wife comes up to me at a party and says, "Dammit, Thurber, stop writing." She usually catches me in the middle of a paragraph.' For 'natural', maybe one should read 'persistent'. The person with this psychology is likely to look at the unique qualities of what readers can do with words on screens, and the way in which different buttons control the way the pages turn. The hard worker is likely to have a good grasp of all the different outcomes of a branching hypertext and will be able to plot, plan and structure while keeping the natural fluency of the forward movement alive. Hypertexts are not necessarily stories, and some writers are creating works for which there is no genre category: they are not quite stories; not quite commentaries on ideas or the world; not quite poetic discoveries. This, it seems to me, is the most interesting area of web writing and the one in which the natural/hard-working writer will succeed.

The wicked child

This kind of writer relies on 'kiss-and-tell': someone who exposes family relationships, friends, acquaintances (or even, like Philip Roth, a whole tribe) in a more or less disguised fashion. 'For most people the first book is about the family, if only metaphorically, and it must be conquered as surely as the walls at Jericho.' But the writer has to be brave and face up to whatever repercussions this may have in terms of personal relationships. Lack of courage may simply add to the already toppling pile of well-written manuscripts that make no particular impression and are 'so well-behaved that they are seen but not heard'. And as an erstwhile Reader for Penguin myself, I can endorse that most novels fall into the per-fectly-competent-but-nothing-special category. The child as writer is a Freudian concept, but those who can transform their own problems into universal experience will get published. Observation of writing on the web suggests that this is the largest class, as the proliferation of *blogging* proves (*see* also pp. 52–6). While this can offer solace to the person writing, it is arguable whether the work itself is any more than personal therapy. As I have said above, a reader is only looking for those who can transform their own problems into universal experience.

The self-promoter

The self-promoter will do anything for fame – there are many such writers today, but it is a shock to realise that Walt Whitman shamelessly trumpeted himself from the roof-tops and sucked up to celebrity writers of the day. But then, he got heard during his lifetime, whereas Emily Dickinson died with 2000 unpublished poems. The self-promoter may grab the media, and sometimes, as in Whitman's case, has the talent to justify the size of their ego. Stephen King's serialisation of *The Plant* (*see* page 17) was one such attempt. Jeannette Winterson also uses the web for personal puff – but neither of these writers is exploring it as a new medium in its own right.

The neurotic

This writer makes a great fuss about the process itself. Writing has to be done with an HB pencil, or on lined paper of exactly the right width, or in Microsoft Word, or only in the mornings, or only when no-one else is in the house, or kick-started by a pot of black coffee. Few of these quirks are as eccentric as Dame Edith Sitwell's, who needed to start the day's work by lying in an open coffin, but every reader will recognise such stalling techniques. And, asks Lerner, 'Do writers develop phobias or are they phobics to begin with?' – a question to which she gives a number of balanced replies, none of which completely answers my own unnerving suspicion that a writer *does* need a touch of psychosis to be truly creative. Many live in the world of chatrooms, personal journals and home pages and are generally writing for an immediate circle or for vanity publication. The web is full of them and part of our problem, as readers, is that quality control is only partially invested in publishing houses and trusted recommendations. For the most part, the general public finds itself awash with fictive offerings and very little guidance on branding.

The purpose of categorising authors in this way is not to push them into a set of five moulds, but to provide an insight into ways in which writing operates and to enable writers themselves to weigh up how they relate to their fellows. Insights into why each of these different 'types' succeeds applies just as much to the electronic world as it does to print.

The web is not, after all, a functional genre; it is, in essence, a publication medium. It needs competent writers and editors as much as it requires technological resources. Setting up a website is neither expensive nor difficult – anyone can do it; but fuelling it with good or exceptional content takes a much more continuous commitment, which few people achieve. The key, perhaps, is to realise that everything we have learned from the print world also applies here. Creative writing using the web is in a continuum. All that is different is that the web opens up the world to more people. Yet, the fact that it is easy to publish does not mean it is easy to write something that people will want to read. Admired writers transcend their own experience.

Lifelong learning

In fact, the ability to transcend your own experience through writing – to move beyond a personal need for self-expression to the universal – is very rarely an inborn talent. Most people need to acquire some skills. Whether these skills are taught at school, in universities or through online and offline writing workshops will depend on the desired outcomes. Writing for traditional publication is only one of an increasing variety of reasons to engage in developing writing skills. Creative writing features at all levels of lifelong learning, from encouraging small children to express themselves during literacy hour and elsewhere, to writing workshops, adult educational courses and higher degrees which have been steadily expanding in recent years (*see* the listing in Part 3).

A new genre, like writing for web display, requires as yet untried skills. It is perhaps why those who do it tend to form support communities to test new ideas against each other and see if they work. Such writing communities become self-coaching venues, where members critique each other's work. There is a value in that, though some may say there are dangers in what sometimes becomes 'amateur therapy'. It is not the purpose of this book to make value judgements on when creative web writing is art and when it is therapy, but it *is* important to flag up that the existence of chatrooms, and of two-way emailing in relation to works posted on a web space, creates blurred boundaries between the two. That is something which web writers celebrate – not deplore – and so those of us with preconceived notions about 'good' or 'bad' writing may find we have to go into a different mode; to engage in new forms of writing freed of previous conceptions.

The same question (of art versus therapy) arises whether writing is on- or offline; but for the individual, such a question is probably irrelevant. It should not be forgotten that the value to individuals and groups of collective explorations and expression is increasingly recognised as a way to psychic and even physical healing. The Medical Foundation for the Care of Victims of Torture, for example, has a 'Write to Life' programme which enables survivors of traumatic and crippling events to work through their disjuncture through stories and poetry. The writer-in-residence, Sonja Linden, says it is about enabling those who come to her to find a voice – not just to record their experiences, but also to transform their relationship to those experiences through the interplay of memory and imagination. She says:

> The main motivation for people who have suffered is to write an account of what happened to them, as a record and as a psychic release. Writing can give coherence to what feels like an incoherent life. And just as refugees need to tell their stories, for important historical and psychological reasons, we need to hear them, as part of our recognition and adjustment to living in an increasingly heterogeneous society. I have found that there is an interconnectedness between writing to heal and making that writing public, having a voice and having it heard, that has huge social, emotional, psychological, artistic and political significance for the age we live in.

The web, of course, provides an ideal venue for the testimonial aspect implicit in this need to explore and process the past or present through the medium of writing as a means of moving into the future. The emergence of personal writing on the web proves the truth of that, whether for curative reasons or to discover oneself and the world through writing. For instance, the enormous popularity of web-based diaries (known as 'blogs' and described on page 52) shows how widely the medium of the web has been seized upon for individuals to affirm their own existence by publicising their interests, activities or passions. Not only that, but the traffic on personal sites shows that people *are* interested in each other's writings about their lives. Some of the reasons for this are explored in Chapter 3.

We have long known that imaginative play in childhood and the fulfilled adult's capabilities exist in a creative continuum, as necessary to the artist's studio as to the engineering workshop and the managers' boardroom. Making room in one's life for imaginative 'play' with writing is something that writers, educators and business organisations all welcome. A number of company-funded initiatives, such as the WH Smith 'writers in schools' schemes, encourage children at primary and secondary level to engage with professional writers in a way which makes them understand that writing is something to take pains over and take pride in. The adage, 'Get it writ, then get it right' puts 'correctness' into proper perspective – that of serving communication and meaning rather than cutting it dead with red-pencil comments. Government-funded schemes, too, backed by the Department for Education and Skills (DfES), recognise the value that self-esteem in creative productivity can bring in developing the best environment for learning, enhancing skills, team spirit and personal development.

If creative writing were simply serving the ends of self-expression, with various communication skills as a by-product, it would have its place at all levels of education. However, there is much more at stake than that. Creative writing, seriously and systematically pursued, is a powerful tool for developing the right and left hemispheres of the brain; fusing the creative with the intellectual. Hence it has an important educative role in developing real learning. The vigour of both postgraduate and undergraduate Creative Writing degrees (as opposed to the stasis or even decline of the traditional English departments) is testament to the seriousness with which this relatively new discipline is being taken. Susanna Gladwin, who initiated one of the first Creative Writing degree courses in the UK (at Middlesex University), notes the significance for personal growth and lifelong educative value of courses such as hers, where individuals and groups learn to take responsibility for a total creative process, and effect change which can be of significance throughout their lives. She says:

> If Socrates is right, that 'the unexamined life is not worth living', then a degree in Creative Writing is not a luxury, as some may wish to think, but a necessity, in its role of renewing the values of a democratic society in its many cultural manifestations. To write, you must read, and read with passion and understanding; to write, you must explore and innovate; seek the most exact, and yet the most daring image; you must observe and empathise. To communicate through writing, you must know the best forms for shaping your ideas, know your market; know your readership and the best tools for reaching it.

The spotlight in Higher Education is moving from teaching to learning. As the web becomes more settled, it can offer an educational venue which opens up this process of *learning through doing* to a wider audience. Writing schools are establishing themselves online as alternatives or additions to accredited degree courses. Schools in the US have pioneered in this field – the New School Online University, New York, being one of many to offer courses in hypertext and in electronic poetry and fiction. The UK is catching up: the Open University offers self-contained units in traditional as well as web-based writing, with all materials available online so that people who live in – or travel to – far-flung places can participate and work at their own pace. The trAce Online Writing School[5], physically based at Nottingham Trent University, places more of an emphasis on interaction between students (as well as tutors) and has been developing ways of making live chat and message boards add value to remote tutoring. At trAce you will find an active and splendid resource for exploring creative web writing, from the 'Man Booker Prize' equivalents of e-writing fame to hypertextual theory and practice – as well as courses in textual machines, workshops in non-linear narrative, in a variety of poetic and story forms, and in writing online family history.

New skills

Most teachers of creative writing are comfortable with offering skills for linear, structured writing that is governed by established rules of organisation, grammar, punctuation and style. Certain forms have their own 'unities' – of time, place, voice, coherence and so on. We're on familiar ground here.

The web, however, is potentially disconcerting because it brings chaos into the classroom. We may be looking for a new set of unities in electronic texts – ones which applaud the shifting relationships between verbal and graphic elements. A literate reader of electronic writing is required to develop the ability to discover and manipulate these shifting relationships. A reader of electronic writing is someone who is prepared to make their own stories out of the links of text chunks being offered to them.

This is hard for teachers of electronic writing who are having to learn alongside their students. Perhaps it means that the process of

[5] <http://trace.ntu.ac.uk/school/>

learning about *what* the web can do for writing is taking precedence over discovering what the web can *successfully* do for writing. In the short term, I believe we should not worry about that. There will be time to pick out the raisins when we have thrown everything into the cake-mix.

Those who engage with web writing will achieve best results if they have a certain level of technical and social ability. Knowledge of word-processing is no longer enough. The key requirements involve:

- a willingness to collaborate with others – desirable because best results may be achieved through teamwork between writers, designers and programmers;
- an understanding of multilinear text, story spaces, icons, linking structures, navigational tags and multimedia elements– how to create new dimensions and how to sustain interest in them;
- the ability to use HTML coding, either directly or in a graphical user interface program, and to understand what JavaScript, Shockwave and Flash can offer – or to work with someone who will realise ideas in technical form;
- familiarity with different web browsers – because it is essential to realise that they all behave differently;
- an ability to use search engines;
- a sense of design – because the writer must attend to the appearance of words on screen as well as any images or sounds that enhance them;
- a firm grasp of structure – writers need some level of control to keep their own vision intact, otherwise it can get lost in the chaos of a million different readings.

Above all, the web writer needs to be open to new ways of working with text and technology, and to be willing to play with and evaluate the experimental writing of others.

Part 1

The web genie

For two days after Aladdin is lured by into the cave by his false uncle and shut in there, he remains in the dark, crying and lamenting. At last he clasps his hands in prayer, and in so doing rubs the ring, which the magician had forgotten to take from him. Immediately an enormous and frightful genie rose out of the earth, saying: 'What wouldst thou with me? I am the Slave of the Ring, and will obey thee in all things.' Aladdin fearlessly replies: 'Deliver me from this place!' whereupon the earth opened.

Part 1 of this book is for readers who want to explore creative writing opportunities on the web, without fundamentally changing their current writing habits. It assumes that you do not want to invest the time and money in getting to grips with complicated software; nor do you want to learn programming skills. You also prefer collaborations that are not open-ended – in other words, co-authorship with chosen colleagues, rather than the free-for-all of anyone-can-write-the-next-chapter. But you do recognise that some partnerships with web designers and technical experts is necessary. At the very least, a writer whose work is intended for web display needs to be aware of any constraints to take account of them when planning the work.

The first thing to get straight is that there is only one technology which demands no concessions at all, and that is the use of the web to supply print-based materials. But that doesn't really fall into the remit of this book (though Print On Demand is described briefly on pp. 36–8 for the sake of inclusiveness), because we are not talking here about print products at all.

Certain specific genres have been a great success in electronic forms, and these are rapidly displacing printed products. For example, bibliographies, abstracting and indexing guides, citation indexes, dictionaries, encyclopaedias, directories, catalogues, and maintenance manuals for complex systems (like aircraft) work well in digital form. But it is stretching a point to call these creative works. What we are interested in here is fiction, drama and poetry, and how the existence of screens is changing reading and writing.

For everything that the web offers, the reader will be using a screen. And until screens are as efficient reading platforms as paper, the web writer needs to make some concessions to make life easier for the reader. It is important to be aware of the constraints of legibility.

1

Reading on screens

A history of e-literature

Where did it all begin? Who really was the first author or publisher to leap into the electronic dark? Simon & Schuster released Stephen King's novel *Bag of Bones* in print and electronic formats in April 1999, followed soon after by *Riding the Bullet* in electronic form only. A year later, King experimentally self-published *The Plant* in e-format, following on Dickens's 'penny dreadful' technique of offering a chapter at a time. Readers paid a dollar a chapter, on an honour basis. At the time, King was said not to have made any money on this, but later reports suggest that he netted around $500,000 – though undoubtedly more than 500,000 separate chapters were downloaded (and perhaps read). While his was possibly the first 'name' that meant anything to the public, in fact electronic publishing dates back roughly 30 years before that.

Michael Hart, who initiated Project Gutenberg in 1971, claims to have invented e-publishing – the only electronic text he'd heard of, prior to the ones which he released, being a religious document from the 1940s. In reality, in Project Gutenberg Hart was creating an e-text archive of already printed (public domain) works; but he did recognise that the computer could replicate textual works and make them instantly available. At first these were very primitive, using capital letters and scant punctuation because the early computers couldn't do lower case. As sophisticated scanning techniques grew, it became easier and more reliable to digitise creative works. Added to that, was the searchability across a wide range of texts which was useful to literary scholars. There are now several mirror sites carrying Project Gutenberg texts[6]. The UK 'competitor' is the Oxford Text Archive[7], founded in 1976 by Lou Burnard, and originally only for

[6] <http://promo.net/pg/>, <http://gutenberg.net/> and <http://gutenberg.org/>
[7] <http://ota.ahds.ac.uk/>

academics in the arts and humanities to 'collect, catalogue, and pre-
serve high-quality electronic texts for research and teaching'. When
I first came into contact with it in the late 1980s it also held in-copy-
right works – for use only in textual analysis, not for distribution.

Neither of these two text repositories used the web at their
inception – possibly, they did not even realise its potential. Users
had to acquire floppy disks (of a size no longer in use) by post.
Publishers also started producing books on disk or CD, which we
called 'floppybacks' and which have vanished without a trace.

One idea that didn't catch on was Alan Kay's Dynabook, which
was a precursor of today's modern notebook computers. Kay was
developing this in 1981, when personal computing technology was
still in its infancy, and it was to include such features as a flat panel
display and wireless communications. The trouble was, he picked the
Apple Newton as his platform. Those who remember the Newton
will recollect that it was a forerunner of the Palm Pilot PDA, but
never gained a hold on the market. Alan Kay is not a household
name, but all computer users are indebted to his early work on the
development of graphical user interfaces. Every time you open a new
window or double-click an icon, you are using Kay's concept.

Developments were slow because the technology was very primitive. In the mid-1980s, when individuals could afford to buy them,
computers typically had 64K of memory, ran at 4.77 MHz, and had
floppy drives of 160K capacity. Most monitors displayed 80 characters by 24 lines of text, graphics were rare, and colour was very
expensive. In 1987, Eastgate – now a flourishing purveyor of innovative e-writing – published its first hypertext fiction: *Afternoon, a
story* by Michael Joyce, which became something of a cult item (the
literati of the writing and computer worlds read layers and layers of
meaning into it – for myself, I never saw the attraction). The story
was originally published on floppy disk and is now available on
CD[8]. The story-space software which enabled this hypertext writing is available in an enhanced version (*see* page 139 for details).
Eastgate was an early e-publisher, but it wasn't until the latter half
of the 1990s that e-publishers started to proliferate (*see* p. 30–4).

A snapshot I took of the various platforms in 1995 shows a number of quaint names that have since disappeared from view. This
should give us pause in trying to predict what will happen over the
next seven years, though it is noticeable that most of the 1995 technologies had shifted to the web by 2002.

[8] <http://www.eastgate.com/catalog/Afternoon.html>

Publishing platforms

Type of publishing	Technologies in 1995	Technologies in 2002
Optical text publishing	CD-ROM, optical CD	Web, CD-ROM for manuals only, DVD
Online and network publishing	database, electronic data retrieval systems	Web and Intranet
Multimedia publishing	CD-I, CD-TV, CD-ROMXA, DVI, Photo-CD, Sega CD, Nintendo CD, SMSG, MPC, 3DO, Full Motion Video	Web with Real Video, Real Audio, Windows Media, QuickTime, MP3, MPEG, AVI, 3D modelling, Flash, Java, Jazz, Shockwave, PlayStation and games consoles
Floppyback publishing	full-text on disk	Web
Hand-held books	Sony DD-20B, Franklin DBS, PDA solid-state, smart card	Rocket eBook Pro, Franklin eBookMan, iPaq, Jornada, REB, MyFriend, GoReader, Davtel t.boook, hieBook, Xinhua e-book, Microsoft Tablet PC, laptops

The consultancy firm, Accenture, predicted that by 2005, e-books will make up ten per cent of all book sales. Is that enough to ensure the survival of e-publishing?

Screen resolution

One of the hard-learned lessons from the past is about paper, ink, typography and print techniques. All this is replaced now by screen resolution, e-ink and e-paper, and what we have learned over several hundred years still applies – but we do need to think about it differently. The survival of e-publishing depends, in part, on the development of screens, and at the moment we are bound by constraints of both resolution and cost. Screen resolution is the number of pixels (picture elements) on a display monitor. The sharpness of the image on a display depends on the resolution and the size of the monitor. The same resolution will be sharper on a smaller monitor and gradually lose sharpness on a larger one, because the same number of pixels are being spread out over a larger square-inch area.

A pixel isn't really the same as a dot-per-inch on a printer, but it helps to think of them in a similar way. So the resolution and monitor size together determine the pixels per inch (ppi). Most PC monitors are somewhere between 50 and 80 ppi and PDAs rise to 100 and sometimes more. The print page you are reading now is 1524 dots per inch (dpi), a good resolution for comfortable reading. Newspapers are usually set at 300 dpi because that is generally adequate for the kind of skim-reading most people do when reading news items. Nothing electronic rises even to 300 dpi. Although ppi theoretically equate to dpi, it's an inexact comparison because brightness and contrast are as important as resolution, which is essentially smoothing the edges of type fonts. Both count more than dots per inch because what's important is that you see a clear image at any angle and in dim light or sunlight without a change in contrast.

Research claims that people read 25 per cent slower on screens of inadequate resolution than they do when reading a print page. They also need to take frequent breaks to stop their eyes from drying out or being disturbed by the flicker from the light source. A print page is more or less readable according to the quality of the paper, the size and x-height of the typeface, whether a serif or sans-serif font is used, the sharpness of the inking and many other factors. The more 'difficult' a text, the more important it is for the design to make the reading process itself as easy as possible. Edward Gibbon, when he was writing the *Decline and Fall of the Roman Empire*, was so concerned about the look of the page that he rewrote every single last line of a paragraph to make sure that it stretched more than half-way across the line length, because he thought that club lines (one or two words at the end of a paragraph) were displeasing and therefore would irritate the reader.

After all a mistake authors so easily make is to assume that the reader is hanging on to their every word in any case. As Robert Graves and Alan Hodge remind us[9]:

---

[9] *The Reader over your Shoulder*, Jonathan Cape, 1943

> How much of the averagely interesting book is actually read by the aver-
> agely interested person? It can only be a small part, and of that small part
> a good deal is lost because, though the eye goes through the motions of
> reading, the mind does not necessarily register the sense.

I have my screen set to 1280 x 1024 at 16-bit colour, which means
that I can see about 250 words in a screenful; whereas 800 x 600 at
256 colours only displays 150 words (and those very pixellated and
hard to read). The choice of resolutions in pixels on current-gen-
eration devices are given below, together with the approximate
popularity of each one[10]:

640 x 480 (5%)
800 x 600 (53%)
1024 x 768 (32%)
1152 x 864 (2%)
1280 x 1024 (3%)
(All available in 256 colours, 16-bit colour or 32-bit colour)

96 x 80
WAP phones

160 x 160
PDA screens

To add to the variety, Netscape and Opera browsers display type
smaller than Internet Explorer does, and the Mac generally goes
one smaller than the PC – though it depends on the brand. It can
sometimes be hard to remember that a layout that looks good on
your own screen will look very different on another.

Fonts

On the web it would be completely pointless to do what Gibbon did
with his paragraph endings, because you have no control over the
look of the screen. Even a PDF file (described below) does not fix
the page exactly as it was when designed in a desk-top publishing
system – as it used to do – because the readers can now reflow text
so that pages expand or shrink according to their comfort reading

---

[10] According to The Counter.com

size. Internet browsers also allow users to set small, medium or large fonts and to have default typestyles that over-ride whatever the person who wrote and laid out the page chose. This is for reasons of choice as well as accessibility for the visually impaired. Typography and graphic design is quite simply uncontrollable.

Fonts themselves depend on what individuals have on their own systems, not what you specify on yours. The ones which you can rely on to look good on screens – and which are universally available – are known as 'web safe' fonts[11]:

Andale
Arial
Arial Black
Comic Sans
Courier New
Georgia
Impact
Times New Roman
Tahoma
Trebuchet
Verdana

Some, like Georgia, look good on the screen, but don't print out well and many people require that. Even if you create a print-only version as well as a screen-read version (which is good practice), it is still better to avoid non-standard fonts. For continuous reading in print, serif fonts (as used on this page) are thought to be more readable. On screen, the opposite is true and a font like Verdana gives a clearer, more readable image. This is because serifs, instead of carrying the eye forwards as they do in print, are so pixellated that they impede readability.

Readability

The eyes don't read; they move across a line of print in a series of jerks and pauses. During the pauses, the eyes take a 'photograph'. When the eyes come to a full stop, the brain organises the photographs so that the message makes sense. If the brain comes across something it doesn't understand, it will instruct the eyes to

---

[11] Downloadable from <http://www.microsoft.com/truetype/fontpack/default.htm>

're-photograph'. If this happens a lot, the reader will give up and move on to something else.

Reading on a computer screen is a not the same as reading from print. For the latter, we have come to rely on a wide range of skills, such as holding a book or journal at a comfortable angle, scanning from left to right, and observing section headings and page layout to distinguish important information. We are also very adept at turning pages and scanning backwards and forwards through them to find specific or half-remembered bits of information. Where there is a research need, people will have several books or magazines open at different pages and are very quick at navigating between them – usually using both hands. All this affects the speed of reading, the length of the pauses, concentration time, skipping, skimming or re-reading and eye comfort. Most people have subconscious strategies for reading that are possibly acquired in childhood.

By contrast, reading on the web is slower. Conventions have not yet emerged, partly because a full generation has not yet grown up who are reading either for work or for pleasure on screens. Nor has the technology caught up, even where individuals do report feeling comfortable with screens. Response time for computers moving on to a new page can be cumbersome (especially with the graphics-rich pages of some experimental works), and navigation is controlled by dragging or clicking with the mouse. Quite often, in order to move about between different electronic windows, the user has to try to find the right one from an overcrowded task bar, or close or re-size some windows. Some hypermedia works open up windows within one another, like sets of Russian dolls. These tasks, being one-handed, mean that navigation is performed serially rather than in parallel with other activities and therefore slows the reader down. As we will see in Part 2, some writers *want* their readers to slow down, but presumably not because the technology is cumbersome, nor because their visual attention is being distracted by some task.

It would be a little easier if we had low-cost, book-sized screens with technologies that can deliver web pages without using cabling, plugs and sockets and telephone wires. These things do exist (they're known as Airport and Bluetooth), but they are too expensive for mass take-up and the radio signalling system does not operate in enough venues to give complete reliability. Therefore, readers today will face problems. It is said that, in the short term at least, screen displays of extended texts will be more successful if they use book metaphor conventions – retaining contents pages and bookmarks, for example, even if there are adequate interactive links elsewhere.

From the above, it can be seen that before creative writing on the web can flourish, the writer has to admit to starting at a disadvantage. Book- or journal-length writings that have an unfolding narrative require a 'fine wine' approach to design style and readability as opposed to the 'quick-glug' fix of supermarket plonk. If you want your readers to savour the reading experience then you have two choices: stick to print, or reconsider what the reading experience is and how you can write differently for it. This will be developed more fully in Part 2.

Having said, then, that it is harder for people to read on screens, what exactly are the choices?

e-Formats

One of the problems for authors of electronic texts is the number of different formats available. In a traditional publishing model, the author can rely on the publisher to make the appropriate deals that are right for the kind of work they are offering. However, traditional models may not be the way of the future, and the savvy author will get better deals, and maximise opportunities – so it is useful to be as familiar as possible with the different formats in this rapidly changing arena.

There are perhaps four types of e-format and a mix-and-match system of different distribution models, described below. Some electronic texts are destined for e-books and others are master files for Print On Demand (POD). The end-result is different, but for present purposes I am treating them as two sides of the same coin.

Electronic formats

Dedicated book-a-likes

These are the *e-readers* – book-sized electronic devices with LCD display screens, search buttons, and different ways of bookmarking and page turning. They weigh as much as a heavyish paperback, cost anything from £70 to £400 at the time of writing (except you can't readily get one outside the US), hold about a dozen titles in memory, and last for 12 hours or so on charge or on battery. One feature of all of them is that they 'remember' where the reader left off and return to that point when you next switch on. They also let you make notes with what one wit has called the Portable Erasible Nib Cryptic Intercommunication Language Stylus – or PENCIL.

Contenders (as I write) include the Rocket eBook Pro, Franklin eBookMan, iPaq, Jornada, RCA REB range, MyFriend, GoReader, Davtel t.boook, hieBook and the made-in-Taiwan Xinhua e-book. The Microsoft Tablet PC is another hardware solution in a different mould. More will come and go before the market settles and someone wins the race to become the standard product. The next technology wave will use flexible e-paper, and its counterpart e-ink, scheduled for 2003 – or whenever someone finds a cost-effective way of producing thin plastic-coated sheets with low voltage batteries so one can roll it into a scroll, and re-use each sheet thousands of times.

Double-function devices

One widely held view is that dedicated e-readers won't capture the market. The buying public might acquire personal digital assistants, acronymed as PDAs, because they have another use as diary and address book. The fact that they are also able to carry e-books is a bonus, but not a reason for buying the device. The main players here are the Palm Pilot, Handspring Visor and Psion range.

Mobile phones come into this double-function bracket too. Unsatisfactory as their tiny screens may seem, there is a growing band of writers who are experimenting with the mobile phone as a delivery mechanism for creative writing. A new acronym language is developing around them. This presents an interesting challenge to writers who are prepared to learn about nodes on the phone cell system and experiment with ways of delivering narratives that change as the user passes from one physical area to another, or to explore ways in which text messaging can deliver stories. Some possibilities involve a blur between reality and fiction. At 160 characters per message (a general maximum), that is a challenge. All one can say at present, is that we cannot discount the idea of mobile phones delivering certain forms of content. Some ideas are to be found on pp. 93–6 in Part 2.

Mobile phone companies are also looking at ways of providing serialised e-books and audio versions of newspapers and magazines over wireless networks. The technological advance they are waiting for is General Packet Radio Service (GPRS) which is very roughly equivalent to being online all the time. The limitations of phone call costs and limited text messaging will no longer apply.

Dedicated software readers

Software solutions – if they are to compete with anything light-weight mentioned above – are essentially for notebook computers.

That instantly cramps the authors' market because PC and Mac hand-helds of acceptable slimness are expensive and mostly toted by the business community. This could have a seepage into academic arenas, but not until the government decides to give every student a reliable lap-top. That said, the software works on full-sized systems too, but, as implied in the section on readability above, who wants to sit upright staring at a computer screen to read a 250-page novel?

The main two contenders are the Adobe eReader and the Microsoft Reader. These are both free, but texts have to be in a proprietary format and are not interchangeable between the readers. Adobe has its Portable Document Format (PDF) which is a universal standard for preserving the original appearance – fonts, formatting, colours, and graphics – of any source document, regardless of the application and platform used to create it. And Microsoft files are in a format known as .LIT (of unknown derivation). Both have their own specially designed readable screen font. Adobe's is CoolType; Microsoft's is ClearType (a French saying with the words *même chose* springs to mind).

Though Adobe and Microsoft are likely to tough it out for supremacy, they are not the only software companies working in this area. Labyrinten is a Swedish company developing software to produce talking books with multimedia content for fully synchronised Digital Talking Books – read by actors and not Stephen-Hawking-like voice synthesis. That's the next logical step and one which promises interesting applications for children's fiction, but it is still in too early a phase of development to be attractive.

Web-based formats

Web-based formats are meant to be read on screen and via any web browser. This is the most diverse of all formats. There are different ways of treating the actual texts (coded, in plain text, or in PDF format already mentioned). And there are a variety of delivery models.

Delivery models

The following models apply to all formats at present – though some experiments with wireless and telephone applications may change the way in which dedicated e-reading devices enable people to buy e-books. At present, content is either in a solid state (like a card or disk), or is encrypted and made available to a particular purchaser or particular dedicated machine with a password. Here are the purchasing choices at the time of writing.

1. **Pay to download** – the book-buying model we are all used to, except that the user then has to decide whether to read it in one of the devices listed above, or print it out.
2. **Buy an electronic text online to read online** (popular for business and professional reference) – the user receives a password and can access the text at any time. This is only viable for people who are online all day at work or at home.
3. **Read the book online free** – but if you want to print a copy you have to pay. This is used for books that most people would want to read off the page – novels, for example.
4. **Download and read free** – this is a promotion model of which the most famous example is *Unleashing the Idea Virus*[12]. This is downloaded free on a daily basis and yet sells in ten languages in hard copy, adding significantly to author, Seth Godin's wealth. For most would-be authors, however, this is the vanity model.
5. **Read a sample; buy the rest** – this is designed to allow users to look at the titles, read a chapter or some sample poems and then go on to make a traditional hard-copy purchase.
6. **Time-based permit edition** – download an e-book paying $1 for 10 hours (cumulative reading), after which the book's 'time-based permit' expires, and the content only available if renewed. An experimental idea launched by Rosetta Books which may or may not catch on.
7. **Read and print free** – useful for public domain texts such as the Oxford Text Archive or Project Gutenberg (*see* also pp. 17–18). This is useful for researchers doing search routines across different texts.
8. **Free encyclopaedias** – such as *Encyclopaedia Britannica* which offers some free reference and is supported by advertising revenues. There's an enhanced service without advertising for those who pay for a subscription or who own the CD-ROM. The free edition may not survive, as advertising on the web is not proving as lucrative as the publishers expected. It is already less expansive than it was when it was first released, and now only offers the beginning of an article with a 'Need More?' button offering complete articles only to premium service members (there's a 14-day trial giving full access).

---

[12] <http://www.ideavirus.com/>

9. **Libraries subscription model** – in which libraries pay a substantial annual fee and the visitors can read and print without further cost. Some examples are the *Oxford English Dictionary, Grove Dictionary of Music,* and *KnowUK.*

10. **Students' texts** – databases of articles and books to which students have access for a monthly fee. One model for this was the American company Questia's academic text repository of books and journal articles in the humanities and social sciences, which folded as I read the proofs for this book. You could search each and every word of all of the books and journal articles in the collection and there were tools that let the student automatically transfer quotes – with citation references in the correct format – into a paper. You didn't appear to be able to plagiarise a whole chapter, which was a mercy, but it was very unclear what the benefits to the original authors were because the deal was with publishers and few authors received recompense. Students paid $10 a month at the time of writing.

11. **Print On Demand** – this is the modern equivalent of short-run presses (more detail on pp. 36–8). A growing trend here is for suppliers to offer mix-and-match chapters across a range of imprints. Travel guides, for example, can be ordered chapter-by-chapter from different books and may then be bound, personalised and delivered. This model could have creative uses for self-publishing authors.

Speed, bandwidth and plug-ins

Bandwidth determines how fast you can download text, pictures and video to your machine. For example, you could download a page of text in one second, but it would take more bandwidth to download a photograph, and consequently would take longer. A colour photograph takes longer than a black-and-white one and size matters. It takes still more bandwidth to download sound files, computer programs and videos than it does text. Virtual reality and 3D presentations require the most bandwidth of all. People don't like watching a blank screen, and research suggests that ten seconds is as long as most people will wait. Standard dialup connections download at around four to five kilobytes a second, so that means the first 20 kilobytes or so need to be interesting enough to grab attention. A short text page with three or four thumbnail-sized graphics will generally load fast.

Broadband connections are changing that because they enable different bits of information to be sent at the same time – increasing the traffic, like lots of lanes on a motorway. Current solutions for the individual user are Cable TV and DSL (Digital Subscriber Line). They are cheaper than metered calls if you use the Internet a lot. True DSL is 15 times faster than the ordinary dialup connection, but domestic versions of it are about a third of that. So your first page could be 100 kilobytes, giving a text page with a bit of Javascript, some menu buttons that change colour on mouseover and a logo.

But it still isn't fast enough, and what we are all waiting for is true broadband using fibre optic cabling that downloads at about 200 kilobytes per second – there's no agreement as to the actual speed. This will allow high-definition film clips, short films, flash animation, three-dimensional video games, video on demand, MP3 files, Internet radio, streaming video, video conferencing and more. A lot of scope for that first page, though to broadcast TV you apparently need between 6-8 megabytes per second of bandwidth.

So broadband isn't here yet. In the short and medium term, the full development of innovative fictive works is held up by this constraint. Experimenters want to use Javascript, Shockwave and Flash as well as video and audio, but if they do they are reducing the size of their audiences to those with high-levels of technology and a commitment to innovation.

The technologies of the web and of all electronic reading devices are still some years away from being able to enhance the reading experience. This means that writers are working within constraints. It may well be, as technologies push further and are driven by wealthy sections of society looking for the next gadget-ridden device, that the technologies writers have at their disposal will always be one step behind the next developmental phase. To be experimental now may involve looking 'old hat' in one or two years (at the time of writing, none of the works I will be looking at in Part 2 is older than five years). When one considers how much energy goes into creative work, it is not surprising that artists are looking for a little more currency than that.

2

New markets

Some people call electronic publishing 'access publishing'. In other words, 'making available or accessible' as opposed to traditional publishing which is 'backing a choice' because the publisher invests in the author. This is because Internet publishing venues can be showcases, bookshops, editorial and design services, and communities. Some read the books they offer to the public and some do not. These are the new e-publishers which are both springing up and vanishing as every month passes. They are all additional to the publishers listed in the *Writers' & Artists' Yearbook* – many of whom have websites and electronic imprints as well as their traditional range – and are listed in Part 3 page 148 ff.

New e-publishers

Among the many Internet venues for new media writers is one called Great Unpublished (listed in Part 3). Like many similar, it is a cross between a community to encourage new writers and a vanity or self-publishing source for Print On Demand. It celebrates being unpublished as a virtue, which is a reversal of the normal perception. A cynical view is that sites like this, offering self-publishing services, stand to make money out of would-be authors who want to see their books in print. But at another level, there is a growing recognition that the conventional publishing machinery has ever-narrowing criteria: in fiction particularly, it is looking for work that falls within limited genre types. Anything that does not have a place within one of the successful big-selling types is risky, and known-brand publishers will be reluctant to put their money into it. It is well-known among fiction editors that there are many, many well-behaved books, nicely written and decently constructed, that will not be missed by the general public if they are not brought to its attention. When your work defies genre categorisation, publishers tend to ignore it because it doesn't fit neatly onto a shelf in a bookshop. Being unpublished does not necessarily mean that a work is inferior, but that it falls outside current publishing sales constraints.

Opportunities, then, exist for exploring some of the genres that do not sell at every station and airport, and for looking at ways in which different media can be put together in non-conventional ways. It is still harder to sell work that steps outside the genre categories, if you want to sell it in conventional form. But if it is conceived with screen-reading in mind – and designed for it – then you stand a chance of appealing to a public that has decided, more or less, what it wants from conventional books but hasn't yet come to any conclusions about what it wants from electronic works – if it rates them at all. Temptations to engage with them grow every month. At the time of writing, three different 'lures' are being put before the computer-owner.

1. Free-till-midnight e-books are arriving with next-day expiry dates and automatic how-to-buy reminders.
2. An experiment with $1 for 12 hours' reading, after which the reader must commit to buying.
3. ePenguins available for the major reading platforms (*see* page 24) and 20% cheaper than their paperback equivalents.

Looking at these in descending order, there is a financial incentive to be more experimental in one's reading. You can't argue with free, and if Cinderella's coach turns into a pumpkin and the book vanishes as you get hooked, then that's all to the good (and a few minutes delay with a credit card or PIN will put it right). The $1 option (equivalent to £1 in UK terms because books are priced higher) is worth a risk, but people will be wary a second time if the first doesn't deliver. And an ePenguin is historically low risk; perhaps the publisher will get more adventurous and initiate ePenguin originals.

A chart of the new e-publishers is included in Part 3 (page 148). In compiling it, I studied each online publisher's site carefully, looking for a submission guidelines page; reading any sample contracts online; looking for the standard royalty arrangements; scouting for download statistics (rarely declared); and taking account of the currency and the look-and-feel of the site. The table is up to date as at June 2002, but this is a fast-changing scene: my advice to authors thinking of taking a project to one of the publishers is to check the site again, and then to enter into an initial dialogue by email. Judge the vibes from that, ask to be put in touch with one of their other authors, and, above all, scrutinise the contract in great detail. If submissions and contract detail are not given online, at least in broad outline, then the chances are that the publisher has something to hide.

Even if you decide that e-publishing direct is not for you, it is instructive to note the wide range of royalty arrangements. Publishers can be seen to be taking commission of between 10% and 90%: there's an argument for saying that 50–50 is reasonable. There is also much good material in some online submissions advice that could benefit any author approaching any publisher.

The Society of Authors has consistently been advising writers to retain electronic rights. Non-exclusive, volume-publishing-only rights make it possible for authors to benefit from sales in other formats. And while some publishers are arguing that 'volume form' does include electronic formats, I think we would dispute that it includes all of them. One could argue the case that a complete electronic text, as laid out in the paper original and saved in desk-top-published format, is equivalent to 'volume', but it's not clear cut with all formats. The case in 2001 between Rosetta Books and Random House centred on Rosetta having bought the e-book rights from authors who owned them because older contracts did not include e-rights. Random House took the view that this was still 'volume' publishing, but the Court of Appeal in 2002 upheld the original verdict in favour of the new e-publisher. The case set a precedent in giving authors, rather than their publishers, the electronic rights to backlist print books.

Submission guidelines

The chart on page 149 ff indicates which e-publishers have submission guidelines – the better ones usually do. These may be in FAQ form, or on an 'Author' area of the site. If you type 'guidelines' into the site's search box, you may or may not find them. Try other likely alternative links.

It is essential to read the guidelines of any publishing house to whom you wish to submit. This is such obvious advice, you'd think it went without saying. Not so. My publisher friends all tell me that the most common cause for rejection is that the author has not paid attention to the guidelines. Either they have submitted a work which falls outside the stated range of the publisher, or they have ignored the basics of how the publisher prefers to deal with a submission. This wastes everyone's time. It is far better to make a personal checklist of what the submission guidelines ask for, and tick off whether you have supplied each item or not. Publishers are not waiting to receive your book, and they will give preferential attention to those submissions which comply most sensibly and considerately with their guidelines.

Your list will probably include these elements, although it won't necessarily be limited to them:

- What sort of fiction, poetry, drama or non-fiction are they looking for?
- Do they specify what they do *not* want? (Many online publishers do make this clear.)
- Do they want completed book-length texts, or proposals in synopsis form with a sample page or chapter?
- How have they asked you to put forward the initial idea and is that what you are doing?
- Are they prejudiced in favour of computer-literate authors who can submit modern word-processing files (Microsoft Word, Word Perfect, RTF, PDF)? Supposing that you have a more antiquated system; what sort of a problem could that be?
- If they request a paper copy (and you might want to ask yourself why, if they are e-publishers), then have they asked for return postage?
- Is there a style sheet detailing whether the text should be single- or double-spaced, what the margins should be and so on?
- Do they suggest how you should name your files?
- What format should any illustrations be in, and do they say who should clear the permissions on these?
- Is there an email contact for further information?
- Have they suggested a covering letter or email about yourself (and if you can't make yourself seem interesting, why should an editor want to read your book)?

Submitting work to an e-publisher is no different in essence from the way in which you would approach a traditional publisher. There is simply no point in offering work to an agent or a publisher if it isn't right for their list and if it does not comply with their own submission terms. Anyone who has to 'sell' a project to the publishers and sales representatives really has to believe in it in order to champion it. It is a little easier in e-publishing because the investment is not so great – but the principles remain the same. The *Writers' & Artists' Yearbook* has further advice on submitting work and it is worth extrapolating from this to the e-book world.

What's in the contracts?

In addition to author guidelines, a good e-publishing site should include a sample contract outlining its general terms. You may be able to negotiate on certain specific points and it is always a good idea to seek advice before signing any contract. Remember, it does have to be signed in handwriting: there isn't yet a system to cope with digital signatures.

Traditional publishers' contracts run to several pages as they take into account every eventuality (*see* *Writers' & Artists' Yearbook* for detail on this). For online contracts, look out for the following in particular:

- Make sure the e-publisher is requesting the non-exclusive right to publish the work in digital format. You should be free to sell it elsewhere in a form that does not compete with it.
- Be wary if the contract requests the rights to any electronic format, and especially if it says: 'including, but not limited to: computer disk, databases, CD ROM, and any and all other computer and computer-related or digital-based storage medium, known and unknown'. It is unwise to sign away any unspecified rights to technologies not yet invented; license narrowly.
- Establish that you will retain the copyright and under no circumstances assign it to the e-publisher.
- Make sure you are happy with the royalty rate (see the chart on pp. 149–158 for the variations – 50–50 is considered a reasonable split between author and e-publisher, but it depends on the circumstances).
- Check what 'out-of-print' means – whether work is deemed to be in print as long as a copy could be downloaded from the site, and, if so, if you can terminate the contract whenever you wish (*see* also below).
- If the contract has a fixed term, try to limit it to between one and three years – this is long enough in the experimental area of e-publishing.

If there isn't a contract at all, but a general 'friendly' understanding, be careful. It could turn out that a higher-profile publisher might want your work, but only on the condition that they acquire first-time rights. It could be argued that availability on a website is seen as first publication – even if no money changes hands and it is simply showcasing.

Self-publishing

In the US alone, where creative writing courses began, there are now apparently 23 million people who consider themselves to be authors (according to The National Endowment for the Arts in Washington). Perhaps the same number, doubtless more, consider themselves to be photographers.

The use of these words – 'author' and 'photographer' – have become democratised because superb equipment is available to all at low cost. Yet with a good eye and reasonable technical know-how, it is much easier to be a good photographer than it is to be recognised as an 'author'. The word 'author' carries some authority to it that contains the respect and recognition of others. Being published used to supply that authority (the brand name of the imprint giving it the appropriate cachet). Now, we have a two-tier system where the traditional values still apply, but are being challenged by those who see a 'dumbing down' in traditional house publishing, where huge advances are being paid by top publishers like Penguin for the memoirs (no doubt ghosted) of temporary celebrities.

By contrast, web-publishing opportunities make it possible for writers with non-mainstream talents, and no notoriety or fame, to find an audience. Whether they call themselves 'writers' or 'authors' in this new world is a matter for discussion. What they are deprived of, through lack of a known imprint, is the power of the marketing machine. And as any traditionally published author knows, this is what truly creates success.

Or is it? There are plenty of examples in history of successful self-publishing ventures. In 1855, Walt Whitman published the initial 12 poems of *Leaves of Grass* at his own expense and was instantly welcomed into the canon by Emerson, who wrote to him saying: 'I am not blind to the worth of the wonderful gift of *Leaves of Grass*. I find it the most extraordinary piece of wit and wisdom that American has yet contributed.' Whitman, not slow to take advantage, had these words – a blurb, as we would now call it – gilt-embossed onto the second volume of his book (presumably before Emerson had read what it contained). This endorsement was seen by the Boston press of the day as, 'the grossest violation of literary comity and courtesy that ever passed under our notice'. How times have changed! And yet, as was noted in the Introduction to this book, it is interesting to contrast Whitman's chutzpah with Emily Dickinson's self-effacing modesty. Writing at much the same time, she appears to have fallen at the very first rejection slip, leaving just under 2000 unpublished poems to be discovered after her death. It's tempting to suggest that real talent will out, no matter how active a self-promoter the author is; but at least poets of today can go beyond the first unappreciative critic and reach an audience during their own lifetime.

One of the most renowned self-publishing ventures was the Hogarth Press, founded in 1917 by Leonard and Virginia Woolf, and originally intended as a diversion for its founders as well as to publish Virginia's own works. It began with a small hand press in the dining room of the Woolfs' home, Hogarth House in Richmond, Surrey and gave an audience to new and experimental works by then relatively unknown writers such as Katherine Mansfield, T S Eliot, Clive Bell, Cecil Day Lewis, Robert Graves, E M Forster, Christopher Isherwood, John Maynard Keynes, Vita Sackville-West and others. They were to form the core of the Bloomsbury group. Today, there is a band of 'Nouveaux Bloomsbury' innovators, little known outside their own coterie but admired as being first in their field. These are the web artists whose work I will be looking at in Part 2.

Meanwhile, there's no need for traditional self-publishers to be innovative. Print On Demand is open to everyone.

Print On Demand

Print On Demand (POD) is useful for good-quality paper copies in runs of one to 250, which makes it appealing for self-publishing. There's a set-up cost and a per-title cost, but both are generally lower than the self-publishing options that have been available up to now. POD is an interesting route for authors who don't mind doing their own promotion, offering a potentially viable digital production model to the publishing industry as a whole.

There are a number of models, of which the most attractive is a local bookshop or kiosk that has a machine capable of printing and binding individual copies ordered by a customer – either in the bookshop itself, or from the Internet – to be collected at a local point of sale an hour later. The attraction is low-cost printing, and no warehousing or shipping costs. Authors in some genres may be able to bypass publishers: by the same token, publishers may start to cherry-pick chapters from different authors and put them into a compendium, perhaps with some personalisation of content on a customer-by-customer basis.

But there are still some unresolved problems. The most obvious is the cost per book. A standard format, 6 x 9 inch 300-page paper-back, perfect bound, on reasonable paper and with a full-colour laminated cover will cost around £1 per unit. Add to that:

- editorial and design costs (whether borne by the author or by a third-party publisher);
- conversion to error-free PDF or PostScript digital file;
- the authors' royalty;
- the producers' profit (author or publisher);
- paper, ink and binding costs;
- the distribution mark-up;
- labour and overheads;
- print-machine maintenance;
- wastage and error margins.

It's difficult to quantify all this, but in conventional litho publishing, the sums look something like this (publishers' profit and costs, including warehousing, distribution and pulping, making up the remainder):

Retail price of book	£15
Author's royalties	10%
Bookshop cut	40%
Unit cost	£1

If the unit costs are any higher than £1 for a standard POD book (and at the time of writing they are), then it isn't sufficiently attractive for bookshops to invest in the machinery, staff and learning curve to make it viable. They would have to have the machine running all day to make enough of a profit to make it worthwhile. Although the 'small is beautiful' model looks good to individual authors and buyers, it can't work unless the machines can stack up hundreds of different orders that can run off the machines continuously – and at a bookshop near you. Current thinking is that orders would have to be in the region of 50–100 different titles a day.

The nitty-gritty of POD is about ancillary costs allied to small systems that can operate in a bookshop backroom – notably paper, ink/toner and binding. Paper delivered in UK A4 (8½ x 11½ inches) or US letter size (8½ x 11 inches) will have to be cut to waste for a 6 x 9 inch trade paperback. That's expensive in the long term and the bookshop or print kiosk is likely to want to optimise on paper.

Another issue concerns the grain of the paper, which should be the same all through the book. This is important because if the grain of the paper and of the cover run parallel to the spine on a perfect-bound paperback, then the cover will hinge better and the inside pages stay open more easily. Customers will not ultimately accept books that warp or come apart, so this has to be factored in.

Small POD systems use ink cartridges which (as most authors will know from their own printers) are expensive and don't last long. Industrial printers used for conventionally printed books have hugely lower impression costs than anything currently on the market for the range of Print On Demand machines.

The real crunch-point, however, is the cover, for which binding, lamination and trimming are normally done on dedicated machines. Print On Demand will require an all-through solution for all the finishing so that a bookshop has a fully automated system that is easy to run. In fact, full automation will require a process that starts with the order and spits out a book without any human intervention in between. Developers are coming up with solutions to this, and when they hit the high streets we will all hear about it. But it looks to me to be some time in the future.

All this simplifies huge technical detail in order to show why, while POD is a wonderful idea (and in some quarters a reality), for most self-publishing writers it is not yet a sufficiently settled technology to mean that they can produce and sell one, five or a hundred books. In fact, e-books sold on the web in one of the formats given in Chapter 1 offer a rather less complicated route to the self-publisher.

Out-of-print

Out-of-print is a more complex issue. It is unlikely that any author will have a digital copy of a former work. Corrections, design and late changes occur after the author or editor has delivered the full text, and this means that the author's own word-processor file is not the final version. For this reason it must be scanned in and converted, and to do that with acceptable accuracy requires a sophisticated scanner and two copies of the book with cut spines, merged and assembled in book order. There are two problems inherent in this. With older books, the author may only have one precious copy and may not be willing to cut it up. With newer books, the chances are that the rights have reverted, but the typographical right still belongs to the publisher for 25 years after publication. It's arguable that scanning violates that right.

Reversion of rights is further complicated by the fact that the term 'out-of-print' does not mean anything any more because one digital master is all it will take to count as 'in print'. While this has obvious advantages to the user, it's not necessarily such a good thing for an author. They would be precluded from moving to a different publisher, or from getting their rights back even if there were merely two or three sales a year. A work should not be considered to be 'in print' just because it is available in Print On Demand form.

Protection

The new electronic markets, however, offer less protection than the old. Theft and plagiarism on the Internet are well-documented problems. There are some practical details in Chapter 5 (page 131) on some web-specific steps that writers can take to protect their own work and to make sure they don't infringe on that of other people – even unwittingly. Even without technology, writers have struggled to explain why this happens. Mark Twain describes the process in *Innocent Plagiarism*[13]:

> I had really stolen that dedication almost word for word. I could not imagine how this curious thing had happened. However, I thought the thing out and solved the mystery. Two years before, I had been laid up a couple of weeks in the Sandwich Islands and had read and re-read Doctor Holmes's poems till my mental reservoir was filled up with them to the brim. The dedication lay on the top, and handy, so by and by I unconsciously stole it. Perhaps I unconsciously stole the rest of the volume too, for many people have told me that my book was pretty poetical in one way or another!

This is a memory phenomenon called 'priming' – retaining knowledge acquired on a previous occasion, without remembering the incident – and as we all know, it happens in everyday life. An idea, or a conversation, or something read in a book pops into the mind

---

[13] On this occasion, I do know. This idea and the quotation from Mark Twain come from *Memories are made of this* by Rusiko Bourtchouladzc (London: Weidenfeld & Nicolson, 2002, ISBN 0297643282), and were faxed to me by the indexer of the book, Hazel Bell, who knows of my interest in this area and often sends me interesting tid-bits. However, if one were to footnote the original source of every single idea (even assuming you could track everything back) then the footnotes would probably occupy more space than the text.

and we do not remember where it came from, or having had the conversation, or the book or newspaper. We probably can't protect ourselves or others from priming – it's part of the creative process. Stealing whole chapters or whole works is another matter. That's piracy, even where there is no intention to defraud the authors of their fame and reputation – only of their income (notoriously prevalent in India). The Internet obviously widens the opportunities for piracy quite considerably. There are some 10,000 individual copyright works illegally on the net in e-book form: the box below shows the top ten authors most targeted by Internet pirates at the end of 2001 (from a Reuters report)[14].

Author	Total no. of copies pirated
Stephen King	More than 1600 (e.g. of *Dreamcatcher, It, Misery, The Shining*)
J K Rowling	More than 700 (e.g. *Harry Potter* (all four books))
Terry Pratchett	193 (e.g. *The Colour of Magic, Wyrd Sisters*)
Tom Clancy	51 (e.g. *Red Storm Rising, Patriot Games*)
Douglas Adams	49 (e.g. *Hitchhiker's Guide to the Galaxy*)
J R Tolkein	42 (e.g. *Lord of the Rings, The Hobbit*)
John Grisham	38 (e.g. *The Client, A Time to Kill*)
Iain Banks	23 (e.g. *Complicity, Inversions*)
Irvine Welsh	13 (e.g. *Trainspotting*)
Douglas Coupland	8 (e.g. *Generation X, Microserfs*)

At present, security remains a serious issue that troubles both authors and publishers alike. Options range from preventing text selection (so users cannot cut and paste), disabling reading on screen (so only one print copy can be made) – or, conversely, disabling printing so you can only read on screen – and password-protection so you can sell passwords. These functions are known to be insecure – the Russian company Elmscroft's software AEBPR (an acronym that is deemed to have originated in Adobe eBook Password Remover, but which now innocently stands for Advanced eBook Processor) can

[14] source: <http://www.envisional.com/press3.html>

extract the decryption key, open an e-book and save it in a straight-forward way as a PDF file that can be opened in regular old Acrobat.

Most pirate copies are e-books available as traditional copy-righted paper books that have been scanned and then converted into plain text or one of the e-book formats (*see* page 24). Once downloaded, the illegal e-books can be printed out or read on any e-book reading device. Some of those listed in the box are cracked copies of encrypted e-books, such as Stephen King's novella, *Riding the Bullet* (which was one of the first e-texts offered by an author of international repute). The code was hacked in 12 hours – and what-ever technologies for encryption evolve, there is always someone waiting to crack the code. A best-selling author like King may still get adequate recompense from buyers with a conscience, but such insecurity in the medium is not attractive to professional writers aiming to make a crust from their work. It doesn't matter where writers just want someone – anyone – to read them. Experimental web writers are in a pioneering position: some believe in the freedom of the net, and part of their credo is the widespread appropriation of other texts (I'll return to that in Part 2). Others recognise that because they are aiming at a new and suspicious audience, they need to make their works available online free in order to build up a following.

Part 2

Exploring Aladdin's cave

Aladdin, having grown rich and married the Princess, has gone hunting and the magician has discovered that he has the magic lamp. He buys a dozen copper lamps, puts them into a basket, and goes to the palace, crying: 'New lamps for old!' followed by a jeering crowd. The Princess, sitting in the hall of four-and-twenty windows, sends a slave to find out what the noise is about; she comes back laughing so that the Princess scolds her. 'Madam,' replies the slave, 'who can help laughing to see an old fool offering to exchange fine new lamps for old ones?' Another slave, hearing this, says: 'There is an old one on the cornice there which he can have.' Now this is the magic lamp, which Aladdin had left there, as he could not take it out hunting with him. The Princess, not knowing its value, laughingly bids the slave take it and make the exchange.

If you've read through Part 1, you will notice that technology is good for expanding global horizons, makes it easier to disseminate minority works and adds some functionality to a creative text. Part 1 spoke mostly about how new media make it harder for a writer to write conventionally where the work will be read on screen, but much easier to distribute a piece written for conventional reading to a wider audience.

Part 2 is for readers who are interested in pushing out the boundaries of what words on screens can do. In this, I will be assuming a degree of technical understanding; to participate fully, you need access to the latest computer models and the latest versions of key software packages. You need *not* to be frightened of programming tools or new writing environments. It's best if you keep an open mind on what at first sight may look like gibberish, and if you are willing to engage in the serendipity of seeing a work grow through (sometimes random) collaborations. Those who are members of online writing communities can listen to, or contribute to, interchanges between people as they try to define new fictive, poetic or entertaining ways of looking at thoughts and meaning. Most, I suspect, will want to know, 'Is this an art form to which I could contribute? Does it add to our understanding of life? Could I say something with it that I have not been able to do before?' My hope is that you will have a positive response, because the medium needs people like you to take it on to its next phase.

3

New lamps for old: captions to an exhibition

This chapter is designed as an imaginary exhibition, because that is one way of looking at some events of the past to explore how the web is building on these – reinventing the wheel differently. Should we view web writing as 'futurist revivalist' or 'neo-post-modernist' or 'avant pop'? Are we, like Aladdin's magician, exchanging new lamps for old?

In a relatively short space of time we have come through three major stages in storytelling:

- the oral, in which stories were handed down in families and tribes and were embellished and changed in each telling;
- the written, in which stories are fixed in a literary form with the 'changes' being different 'readings' according to interpretation;
- and now the electronic age, in which stories develop individually by being read in a self-propelling order as well as collaboratively (like oral recitals) where individuals post up their own versions of what happens next. On-screen narratives also use graphics and animations as part of the 'text' – leading to new ways of writing and of reading.

As I said in the Introduction, however, the existence of computers is not fundamentally creating a completely innovative art medium. Much of what is on the web is iconoclastic and is a development of what writers or artists have already tried. The more successful of those working on the web have looked back at some previous experiments to see where the influences behind what is happening today lie. After all, some experimental ideas gained influence while others faded from fame. Rob Wittig, who made his name as an electronic writer in the days of bulletin boards and now runs a web 'literary studio' called Tank20[15], writes (and I'm leaving the spacing

---

[15] <http://www.tank20.com/>

as it appears on his web page, since white spaces for screen reading are his hallmark):

trashy, pop stuff is often later

looked upon

as literature

The less successful web writers are those who actually do write 'trashy, pop stuff' that will never be anything else, because they have misunderstood the difference between revitalising literature by bringing it into the present and the dreariness of the mundane. It is easy to be dismissive of all the web's 'trashy, pop stuff'; there *is* a lot of it about. But it takes a while for the novice e-writer or e-reader to see what the 'serious stuff' is getting at. I think we need to suspend our disbelief, to follow imaginatively and let the mind play. The writers who feel that the web allows them to be free of the prison of the book have not yet found out what to do with their freedom. It may take another five or six years of experimentation to discover it.

The web writers I quote from (with permission) in this chapter and the next are acknowledged among the web 'digerati' as innovators with a serious purpose. I am not – and make no show of – critiquing their work (even if the odd comment is let slip). I have simply chosen a few sample works to contrast what is on the web with their historical parallels. They are not intended as a background to today's creative web – the Society for the History of Authorship, Reading & Publishing, with its massive history of the book project, may achieve that. What seems important here is to demystify web writing by demonstrating that it exists within a continuum. So, just as the futurists brought visual and verbal arts together in an attempt to debunk standard forms, so the web is carrying on that same tradition. The futurists are now lodged well in the past, so much so that their art has a quaint charm and collectors' item value. In their own day they were regarded with as much suspicion as the web is now. It's possible, though it doesn't seem feasible or likely, that we should be preserving today's creative sites for their future antique value.

A book like this one is, of course, at a disadvantage here since the historical examples can be quoted on the static page, whereas their digital equivalents are dynamic. I can give some examples, but they are not necessarily the best, because the web is, after all, adding the new element of movement in time. In that sense, it offers a new space. I simply want to draw attention to the ways in which the new space expresses older forms. In doing that, I ask the reader to imagine this chapter as a type of exhibition presenting some themes with specific examples and captions to put them in context.

In an exhibition space the 'old lamps' of familiar published works would contrast side by side with dynamic screens showing the 'new lamps' of new-media works. Unfortunately, this being standard book publishing, economics do not even allow the luxury of colour reproductions, so the reader will have to use some imagination. I have added some hypernotes to link to places on the web where illustrations may be seen, so giving these static pages some measure of interactivity. We mustn't forget that such new concepts of pushing out the boundaries of the page reverberate back into traditional books as well – even if hyperlinking is, in a sense, a revisiting of footnotes and indexes.

The topics below are the settings in which I have chosen to view a selection from recent web writings. The intention is that these juxtapositions will both provide a continuity and trigger inspirations for those writers who are looking beyond the page.

Illumination

The Psaltery to *Patchwork Girl*

Let's start with the very beginning of textual embellishment: illumination. Please imagine an exhibition space showing the wonderful and precious *Book of Kells*, the *Luttrell Psalter* or any medieval Missal or Book of Hours with the other items mentioned in this section in nearby cases.

When the *Book of Kells* was written, around 800 AD, and for many hundreds of years after, the purpose of illumination was to light up the text (the literal meaning of the word) and to make it easier to read by breaking up the subject matter into blocks of text separated by structural decorations – an early form of paragraphing.

Integrating decoration within the text, as opposed to illustrating it in a separate plate, has been a part of book production ever since, but not until the web have writer-artists had such an exuberant palette of decorative elements, still, moving and aural, to blend into their texts. The cost of such modern illumination is within range, but only at basic levels. The price of software such as Dreamweaver, Photoshop or Flash does not compare with the preciousness of parchment, gold leaf, cobalt blue or vermillion, though keeping up with all the latest versions and getting to know them *is* expensive and beyond the purse of the lone-garret writer. While computing centres and universities give free access, the reality is that only writers who are associated with them can expect to be up to speed with the modern tools. This is having its effect on the experiments in web writing that are currently on view, as they tend to come from people associated with universities or technological units within companies who both have the latest versions of the software and are anxious to encourage and promote their use.

Perhaps because of this, we have not yet found a genius of the stature of William Blake, who stands unique in literature for his outstanding talent in writing, designing, etching, illustrating, engraving, printing, advertising and (occasionally) selling his own work. It was his aim to 'bring high art into the homes of ordinary people in a style more ornamental, uniform and grand than any before discovered'. His illuminated books were a true marriage of word and art and my imaginary exhibition space presents to you any of the *Songs of Innocence* (1789) with their richly decorated calligraphy and vignettes. The various sequences of different copies of *Songs* suggest that there is no one developmental path through the stages of the poems, no single authorised reading. Elsewhere in Blake are marginalia, underlinings and annotations. Is it sacrilegious to suggest that Blake might have been entranced by the web's possibilities? Certainly, he has influenced web writers today.[16]

So too have the Gothic Revivalists in the mid-nineteenth century, who, seizing on anything medieval in architecture and in design, took up illumination again after printing had rendered it obsolete. Like some working today, they aimed at decoration for decoration's sake and it was intended to be admired rather than actually used – the calligraphy sometimes being so elaborate that it is hard to read. They created a fad for visually decorated 'addresses' to mark anniversaries and other special events. Queen Victoria received 2000 of them in her Jubilee year.

A century later, in the 1980s and 1990s, the Royal Academician, Tom Phillips, advanced this to high art in a series of paintings called 'Curriculum Vitae' which are 'addresses' to his own life. On his own website[17] he describes this art form as a sequence of blank verse ruminations with pictorial glosses:

[16] <http://www.blakearchive.org/>

[17] <http://www.tomphillips.co.uk/portrait/cv/>

The central image is of course the text, the commentary in each case being the surrounding pictorial matter, which in some cases is also formed out of text... I regard texts as images in their own right: treated as they are here with words ghosted behind words to form a (literal) subtext they are all the more image for being doubly text.

There is a similar vogue now for personal commemoration on graphics-led web pages where the difference between text and image is being eroded. Much web writing falls within this range and I will consider these 'self-illuminations' on pp. 52–6 where there is more concentration on autobiography and the web. Among them are many e-poets, like Peter Howard[18], who are using Flash animation to create self-portraits within a screen frame.

I would also like to put into my virtual exhibition for this section one of the seminal hypertext works – and one of the few to be making money for its author and for the publisher, Eastgate Systems (one of two or three of my examples not freely available on the Internet, and the only one older than five years). It is Shelley Jackson's *Patchwork Girl*[19] written in 1995. Her more recent work *My Body* (2000) is still drawing on the same preoccupation with writing as a form of shedding one's own skin.

Shelley Jackson studied creative writing at Brown University which has long been in the vanguard of new media writing, just as the East Anglia MA in Creative Writing opened doors to literary writers in the UK.

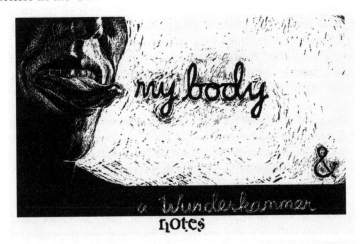

[18] <http://www.hphoward.demon.co.uk/flash/portrait.html>
[19] <http://www.eastgate.com/catalog/PatchworkGirl.html>

This hypertext refers back to its print predecessors: Frank Baum's book *The Patchwork Girl of Oz* (1913) and Mary Shelley's *Frankenstein* (1818), and is an individual rereading of the famous story. It's a quirky choice to place it in the 'illumination' part of my gallery rather than in one entitled 'gothic form' or 'bricolage', but that just shows how inter-referential all hypertext works are. The work is included here partly because it harks back to the monster marginalia of the *Book of Kells* and others, and partly because of its visual treatment of text. It also serves to pin-point how hyperfictions cross boundaries, bringing together different media and breaking down some of the categorisations which have far too long been part of the literary canon.

The work centres on Mary Shelley's monster's never-born female mate, and its central metaphor is the patching together of a new body, of flesh or text, from linked fragments of other bodies – also of flesh, also of text; once dead, now given new, if somewhat strange, form. Early on, the reader learns:

> I am buried here. You can resurrect me, but only piecemeal. If you want to see the whole, you will have to sew me together yourself (in time you may find appended a pattern and instructions – for now, you will have to put it together any which way, as the scientist Frankenstein was forced to do). Like him, you will make use of a machine of mysterious complexity to animate these parts.

The animation – or illumination – is in the hands of the reader. The work is divided, like the senses, into five linked sections, and one of these is the raiding of the graveyard for body parts – and for the stories attached to their previous owners. Footnotes, marginalia, and probable autobiography are part of the hypertext structure. To quote from Shelley Jackson herself:

> You could say that all bodies are written bodies, all lives pieces of writing. First, because our infinitely various forms are composed from a limited number of similar elements, a kind of alphabet, and we have guidelines as to which arrangements are acceptable, are valid words, legible sentences, and which are typographical or grammatical errors: 'monsters'.

Interesting as this work is, it has to be said that the reader needs a great deal of patience and willingness to engage in the experience of following it through, to squeeze from it the wealth of meaning that teachers of hypertext theory have seen in it. The beauty of an illuminated manuscript page has instant appeal, whether you can read the words or not, and whether you can follow through the meaning of every decorative twist or not. The patchwork nature of Jackson's work – and of the web in general – requires a different aesthetic expectation in readers. We have a long way to go before that becomes widespread.

Incunabula

Pamphlet to porn

Discounting bibles, books printed before 1501 are called *incunabula* which literally means 'cocoon; wrapped in swaddling clothes'. These infant printed works were put together by celebrated printers, such as Caxton, Aldus Manutius (from whom the Aldus software publishing products take their name) or Nicholas Jenson – essentially private presses offering pamphlets, flyers, privately circulated or unpublished manuscripts, ephemera and curiosa. The presses defined not just the typography of the printed product, but how it was organised. Much the same is happening now with web designers, who, while not having much freedom with typography (for reasons outlined on page 21 ff, above) are redefining ways in which web *incunabula* are being organised.

All this began in the late 1970s and early 1980s with an information exchange system running via the bulletin boards known as BBS, Fidonet and Arpanet which predated the Internet. This was known as the 'mail culture' and was similar to the Soviet Block samizdat culture. This in turn is nothing new, as the 'chapbook' and 'pamphlet' cultures that sparked so many revolutions, including the American and French, show. Mail culture (and one could have spelled that 'male') spawned a huge variety of oddities, including anarchic art, pseudo-science and techno-occult.

Another similarity between the original *incunabula* and web culture is the preponderance of erotic or pornographic literature and works of various kinds beyond the normal fringes of publishing tolerance. To some extent – though never completely – minority presses specialising in erotica could be policed and controlled in the physical world, but the Internet has made pornography an uncontrolled and hugely successful publishing enterprise. Where ordinary publishers are unable to profit from buying and selling on the web, pornographers have done deals with premium line telephone services and at the time of writing are able to charge £1.50 a minute (more perhaps) for pay-per-view services.

Whatever your own views on this and on censorship generally, a lot slips through the firewalls. For example, if you look in the *Penguin Book of Homosexual Verse* for James Kirkup's poem 'The Love that Dares to Speak its Name', you'll find a blank page. If you want to read the poem, type the title into the Google search engine and you should get to it in less than five minutes (depending on what net-nannying software is on the network you are using).

The Pillow Book

10th century diary to 21st century blog

In 10th century Japan, when *The Pillow Book of Sei Shônagon* was written, the term 'pillow book' denoted an informal diary. The author protests, as do most diarists and makers of journals, that *The Pillow Book* was intended for herself alone. This is one of the earliest narratives and describes the reminiscences of a lady-in-waiting at the court of a Heian Empress and the Japanese court of the time. Yet it is surprisingly modern, also cataloguing her personal thoughts and attitudes and including lists of likes and dislikes: 'Things that give an unclean feeling', 'Adorable things', 'Presumptuous things', 'People who seem to suffer'. If you saw these listings on a personal website now, you'd probably wince, yet a thousand years later they fascinate. Is this rarity value, or is it something else? Surely this is the forerunner of today's 'blog' – frightful word, ancient concept.

A blog is a 'web-log', or web page made up of usually short, frequently updated posts that are arranged chronologically – like a what's-new page or a journal. The original web concept (c. 1998) was that a person kept a diary of their explorations of the web, making it public for others to inspect and follow up. It was within the tradition of writing on the web being self-referential: that is to say, people wrote about what the web meant to them. This is not unlike the many novels and plays that are about writing novels and plays.

By 2001, this had changed and 'bloggers' (those writing web-logs) were not cataloguing the web itself so much as writing their own personal logs, many being physical journeys as well as 'what's on my mind' type wanderings. Many blogs are personal; others are collaborative efforts based on a specific topic or area of mutual interest.

The content and purpose of blogs vary greatly – from links and commentary about other websites, to news about a family, person, or idea, to diaries, photos, poetry, mini-essays and fiction. The offerings are a very mixed bunch. Postings have titles like 'The Adventures of AccordionGuy in the 21st Century' or 'Reality blurred'. Non-fictional uses include 'Art can be neither good nor bad: a personal view', and 'A libertarian reads the paper', in which the blogger posts up snippets of things that he has read in the newspapers and have taken his fancy. The *Guardian Unlimited* makes a virtue of this medium in its variation on the theme – a web-log that is a diary of the best online news, features and analysis.

In fact, it was on 11th September 2001, when New York's twin towers so catastrophically fell, that blogging really came of age as thousands of individuals gave their own perspectives and thoughts on the tragedies of that day. This was personal journalism at an emotional peak: for weeks afterwards the media drew on personal writings, videos and voice-overs. The repository of the 11th September blogs could be said to be a collaborative work of some meaning; a performance installation such as writing had never before achieved.

Some web aficionados claim that the future of web publishing is in blogs. Not only is it a testament to the state of the world, but people, it seems, enjoy cataloguing their lives, interests or random musings and other people like reading them and linking to them. To quote one irresistible way of putting it, 'The other people who have blogs... read your blog, and if they like it they blog your blog on their own blog.' (Rebecca Mead in the *New Yorker*, November 2000.) There may even be an art-form tucked away in blogging – if it can overcome its unfortunate nomenclature.

Blogging is in the tradition of the *Big Brother* voyeurism culture which pervades popular television and which demonstrates that people have an insatiable appetite to spy on other people's lives. There is, it appears, an A-list of internationally known bloggers – known amongst themselves, that is – who get some thousand visitors coming to read the ups and downs of their lives and loves. To get blogged by an A-list blogger, I'm told, is like being chosen for the Oprah Book Club. One enthusiast of the genre has set up an award for web-logs in 30 categories (such as 'theme', 'culture', 'process' and 'character'). In 2002 the prize money for each category was 2002 cents.[20]

[20] <http://www.fairvue.com/?feature=awards2002> (change to 2003, 2004, etc.)

Whatever you, as a reader, feel about this, it is clearly an area of web writing where people can be as creative as they like. Writing classes have long encouraged the writing of a daily log-book as a form of thinking press-ups – it's known to aid fluency and writing confidence, and many authors find daily scribbling both necessary to their creative health and a source of inspiration later. Whether you choose to keep such limbering up under your pillow or publish it to the world, is, of course, an individual choice. Pepys had his own diary so under the pillow that it was in code.

So it is interesting to explore quite what *is* the attraction of writing oneself in web space. The blog only became accessible when the availability of free online software (*see* page 136) made it possible for individuals to post up a daily diary with no knowledge of coding of any kind. You type into a message box, hit a publish button and a timed-and-dated chunk appears on your own website. Before that, some basic knowledge of coding and web functions was necessary and individuals tended to produce a 'home page' which had five or six links to personal interests, pets, family members and so on. Many still exist in static, and often unfinished (or 'under-construction') form. Personal home pages can be seen as reflecting the construction of their makers' identities. Creating such pages offers an opportunity for self-presentation and the web offers an unique context in which to shape a public identity. People do this all the time – the clothes they wear, the books they display, the lifestyle choices they present to like-minded people. The web is the first venue where they can construct portrayals of themselves using words and pictures.

I also see a link between the personal home page, the blog and autobiographical experimental fiction. Here's one that brings in the second meaning of the phrase 'pillow book', which is our current heading – i.e. mild erotica intended to be read in bed. I'm not sure that the winner of the Electronic Literature 2001 Fiction Award would see herself within a tradition dating back to *Sei Shônagon*, but I would like to place *These Waves of Girls* by Caitlin Fisher[21] in the last exhibition case in this section. True, it's hard to read in bed – and that is one of the standard criticisms levelled against e-literature – even though slim-line computers are rapidly making that possible.

This is a shortish work in hypermedia form (she calls it a novella, but I am not sure such terms are appropriate to the web). It

---

[21] <http://www.yorku.ca/caitlin/waves>

explores memory, childhood play, puberty, girlish cruelty, and sexuality. It opens with images of moving clouds drifting across the screen, mingling with the sounds of girls laughing – rapidly devolving into sea-bird-like cackle. Click-links take the reader to what appear to be short autobiographical memories, little stories, rich images, overlapping sounds, anecdotes and meditations from the point of view of a four-year-old, a ten-year-old and a 20-year-old. The female protagonist invites the observer to become a voyeur on her seductive fantasies.

The judges gave it an award because it 'develops a structure that takes advantage of what web-based medium does best – i.e., Fisher creates an interconnected web of branching, narrative possibilities that evoke not just the girlhood of a single protagonist but a broader perspective of girlhood(s)'.

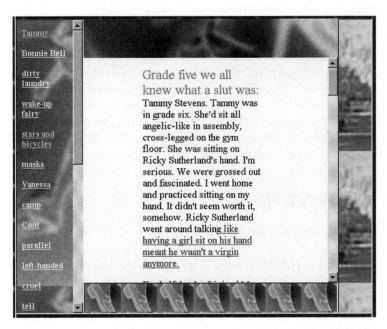

Here is a sample text chunk – not in its own typography, which I feel bound to say does the work no favours. Indeed, almost universally in these experimental works, typographic design seems to be an issue to which the writers have paid scant attention. Each unit is within a scrapbook collage of images and the underlined words lead to other short lexia (defined on page 73) of a similar length:

> <u>Vivian</u> and I run through the marketplace searching for fruit. We wear long skirts we hike up, fists full of cheap cotton. <u>In Fez</u> they call us the little Quebecois girls and no-one bothers us at the entrance to the medina. The ones we like best taste like apple-bananas – they have rows of big dark seeds. We gather these in our mouths, six or seven seeds at a time until our mouths are full of them like smooth rocks. And we spit them hard at the ground and Mohamed, who sells us felt boots, laughs at us, girls full of seeds, skirts up and spitting. We eat the fruit <u>off the end of a swiss army knife fearless, aching</u>, like we've hunted and killed something much more substantial than fruit from a market stall.

Other lexia, many of them sexually aware, are of similar length and enclosed in stand-alone units, and the whole piece relies on a build-up within the reader's mind as the experiences parallel or contrast with their own memories of childhood.

The web works in this section are varied, and – whether hypermedia narratives, interactive scrapbooks, sophisticated mission statements or personal web pages – offer new ways of answering the time-honoured question so fundamental to creative writing at all levels: 'Who am I, and what am I doing in this world?' It will be up to the writers of the future to develop this question further and meld it with the new media opportunities in ways that give real meaning and appeal for others.

Epistolary fiction

Letter-writing and travellers' tales

Another genre that is reinventing itself on the web is the epistolary novel, which is traditionally written in the form of a series of letters exchanged among the characters of the story with extracts from their journals sometimes included. (Our imaginary exhibition can refer back to Mary Shelley's *Frankenstein* here.)

Whole books and theses have been devoted to the appeal of this genre and to the collusion between author and reader that is at the heart of it. Since the plot is not directly told by the author, the reader becomes an eavesdropper and as a result is somehow implicated in the unfolding of the story. You wonder, should you be listening in on this private correspondence – and at the same time you know that the author has reasons for feeding bits to you a scrap at a time. Richardson's *Pamela* (1740) – sometimes heralded as the first modern novel – follows this form. And in my imaginary exhibition, I would put the Epistles of St Paul in the first exhibition case just as a reference token to the origin of the word 'epistolatory', followed by examples from Trollope, Jane Austen, Alice Walker in *The Colour Purple* and many other novels in letter-writing form in the intervening centuries.

There are a growing number of online narratives which use emails extensively. Some give you access to a fictional email account where you can read sent and received emails; some are sent to you as real emails; others have been sent out as a performance of sorts, but are now only browsable as archives.

One of these is *Online Caroline*[22], which could come into a number of sections in this book as it is part web diary, part web-cam film (*see* also page 97), and part email. It is archived now, but it won a BAFTA award for the interactive category in 2000. The interesting thing about it from our point of view here is that the visitor fills in a web form (or questionnaire) on their first visit and then receives personalised emails as the 24 episodes of the serial unfold. These emails are generated from the information you give in your answers to the questionnaire (name, interests, and so on) and are partly reminders to the visitor to go back to the site for the next episode. The emails give the illusion that visitors are part of the story. In fact, as Tom Harvey (who was on the development team) told me, the underlying story is the same for all visitors. You think you are interacting with it because it is tailored to you, but actually you are being manipulated. Harvey's experience with this project led him to believe in narratives that proceed by personal email with filmic elements online. And, as he graphically expresses the predicament of web authors waiting to pounce on a new genre, 'The Early Christians get the best lions.' The only problem for those of us waiting to pounce is that writing is a one-man activity, but if the future is in using web cams and film elements then we will need to form collaborative teams. To get ideas, try the archived version, but you can't play unless you sign up first – because that's where the personalising originates.

Another experiment with email narrative is Rob Wittig's *Blue Company* at Tank 20's Chicago-based literary studio[23]. The concept was that a man sends emails to his beloved and she forwards them

[22] <http://www.onlinecaroline.com/>

[23] <http://www.tank20.com/>

to her friends – the people who sign up to this (that's you, dear reader). The 2001 postings were archived as I write, meaning that you can read them consecutively, but without the time delay combined with an invasion of your inbox which changes the genre from a tightly controlled story progression by letters to an episodic delivery to your email doormat. A 2002 performance should be in progress by the time this book is published.

My 'lamplight' exhibition that is forming this chapter, ends this section with the epistolary genre of the traveller's tale in the *World of Awe*, which enables subscribers to receive emailed love letters from a traveller once a month until 2003[24]. This project is endorsed as part of the 2002 Biennial Exhibition of the Whitney Museum of American Art, and deserves some attention because new media narrative and art projects are relatively new to the museum's portfolio of interests and illustrate a trend towards encouraging the writer-cum-artist which will be welcomed by readers of this book.

World of Awe was conceived by the artist-writer Yael Kanarek (in collaboration with software designers) and explores the connections between story-telling, memory and technology. The traveller's lap-top is found abandoned with a series of love letters on it, written in the style of magic realism. According to the site, the email delivery service 'expresses the capacity of the Internet to reappropriate and recontextualise artistic content'. While the web requires a person to visit, an email reaches out, thus enhancing the sense of personal intimacy to the threshold of eeriness.

It's true that viewing a web page and reading an email are two different events, and web writers of the future may continue to respond to these differences in interesting ways. There's another twist to it in the section on games below (*see* pp. 87–9) and I think that this 'emailolary' fiction may grow. And travellers' tales find another parallel web writing in works involving maps and imaginary countries which provide starting points for some of the student exercises in starting to write interactively.

---

[24] <http://www.worldofawe.net/>

Narrative

Tristram Shandy, Borges and Fibonacci

The word 'narrare' in Latin means 'to tell a story, to relate' and is etymologically connected to 'gnarare' which means 'to know'. This suggests a connection between knowing and story-telling which is evident in everyday life. Small children love to be told stories that they know – and are unforgiving if any known elements are left out or changed in any way. Greek tragedies (which informed so much of the development of modern drama) also depend upon the watcher knowing the story beforehand, joining in the observations of the chorus as they comment on the action. The Victorian novel moved the reader forwards by giving out authorial confidences, so that the reader would have more knowledge of possible outcomes before the characters in the story acted out what the reader foresaw would happen. Readers, audiences, and writers collude in a sharing of disparate levels of knowledge, which is the well-known ploy of using dramatic irony from which a plot and its denouement get their meaning.

The web literati, however, avoid or evade traditional narrative ploys, and that challenges the reader's expectations. Story-telling is constantly reinventing itself – as it has through all the ages. For our exhibition here, I offer the named items below.

The convention that narratives ought to move forwards in time, not backwards or sideways, and that the beginning ought to predate the end was subverted as long ago as Laurence Sterne's *The Life and Opinions of Tristram Shandy* (1759-67) which is often referred to as the forerunner of non-linear writing. The notion that our personal experience of time is not linear but diffuse is embodied in stream-of-consciousness novels like Virginia Woolf's *The Waves*, James Joyce's *Ulysses* and many others.

The development of the modern novel has been challenging the notion that narratives require serial progression for some time. Even writers of biographies today eschew the convention that their narratives should start with birth and end with death. As far back as the Victorian age, when reader expectations demanded strong narrative lines with all the ends tied up in a denouement, George Eliot was writing (at the end of *Middlemarch*):

> Every limit is a beginning as well as an ending. Who can quit young lives after being long in company with them, and not desire to know what befell

them in their after-years? For the fragment of a life, however typical, is not the sample of an even web.

The web image is interesting, deriving perhaps in the author's case from weaving, but worth transporting to our own modern web context. She is acknowledging that 'beginnings, middles and ends don't occur in real life. We never reach the point at which all dramatic tension is suddenly resolved and the characters then 'live happily ever after'. In like fashion, web artists are exploring ways in which chapters, paragraphs and sentences do not have a set sequence as determined by the writer, but one in which the readers step through choices with a willingness to find the dramatic meanings for themselves.

Much of the work of Jorge Luis Borges explores this, and it is not surprising that several web writers have used his work as a starting point for work of their own. What is *The Garden of Forking Paths* if not a gift to interactive story-telling? One story in *Ficciones*, 'The Book of Sand', has a narrator who is sold a book with no beginning and no end. It is impossible to turn to the first page or the last page, and the pages in between are not numbered consecutively. There are illustrations, but having seen an illustration once, it is impossible ever to find it again. The book is infinite and non-linear. Borges is playing with ideas about literature and its presentation, ideas about what constitutes 'a book', and in the process he anticipates some of the possibilities of cyberliterature.

So there is a sense in which we have been training ourselves up as readers for non-linear reading for several generations.

This is born out by my next exhibit in this chapter of imaginary exhibition spaces – *The Book after the Book* by Giselle Beiguelman[25].

[25] <http://www.desvirtual.com/thebook/>

I include this because it is a cross between a web fiction and a creative essay on the 'reading/writing net/condition' (and novelists are continually writing about writers writing). Its author (rightly perhaps) seems to be saying that it is impossible to write about non-linear narrative in a linear fashion. So she writes her essay as if it were a fiction, using the experimental ways of deploying words used in the forms of web writing covered in this chapter. This work sees itself as a part of Borges's 'The Book of Sand', playing with text within the screen space. Words do not have to sit still as they do on a printed page; they can flash on and off or follow the movement of the mouse around a screen. They can be black on a white background one moment, white on a black background the next. One phrase can fade off the page, to be replaced by another coming into focus. They can travel from left to right or from right to left. Instead of being printed on a white background they can be laid against a colour; or they can be coloured themselves; or they can be overlaid on top of a picture.

The pipe marks (|) in the quote below indicate line-breaks – time-coding delivers each phrase, a line at a time, to the screen like a PowerPoint demonstration:

| It turns around a bookshelf. | It is impossible to move between its shelves | by means of the browser. | You will always return to an interval. | To move between shelves, | use the navigation bar. | On selecting one of the works, | you will leave this site. | From any point of the site | you can go back to | The Book after the Book index. | Nevertheless, the index does not send | the reader to all pages. | After all, again recalling Borges, | is there a better place than a forest | to lose a leaf? |

In Borges's 'The Book of Sand', we are meant to recall, the narrator hides the chaotic book in the basement of the Argentine National Library, which contains nine hundred thousand volumes, in order to bury it. This raises some interesting questions for up-coming web writers who need to resolve whether the web is a huge library without shelves or aisles, or storeys, offering a huge single text without beginnings or ends, or whether we can cut it down to size.

I remember once attending a lecture by Professor Heinz Wolff (who for the last 30 years has been running a zany contest called the Great Egg Race) in which he demonstrated how the human mind recreates patterns out of chaos. He showed a series of slides. In the first were five coins in dice formation. The second had a handful of other coins thrown on top – still in a recognisable pattern. There were a couple more slides; still showing an arrangement. Then it became too much – there was so much money in the slide that it became a chaotic jumble. But after yet more coins had been thrown on the heap, new patterns started to emerge again until again we had a formation in which five units were distinctly visible. Can the reader imagine those slides in my gallery? And next to them a large Jackson Pollock splatter-painting which will show that what emerges from the seeming chaos is a distinct, though random, pattern.

Looking for pattern is a recognisable theme in web writing. *Fibonacci's Daughter* (2000) by M D Coverley[26] has a strong storyline which the reader has to tease out. It begins with some Fibonacci patterns accompanied by music. Click on the changing patterns and you get the rubric:

Leonardo de Pisa, Fibonacci
(1175-1250)

was a mathematician who codified number sequences and spatial relationships of objects found in nature and used by ancient architects. His book Liber abaci, was influential in the adoption of Arabic numerals.

The Fibonacci numbers are
0, 1, 1, 2, 3, 5, 8, 13, ... (add the last two to get the next)

The golden section and related numbers are:
+ 0.61803 39887 ... and + 1.61803 39887 ...

A picture of a shell offers the only click link, leading on to the next screen:

Fore-word

Even at the quiet, dark end of the Huntington Beach mall, lights flash from the theater marquee, the neon sign in the Buster Brown Shoe Store, the drift of human shadows; the center at night is a cacophony of light rhythms. The sound is country muzak, fall of chunky heels, murmur of discontent. Stores may languish or open and close practically overnight. It is here that I discovered the Bet Your Life shop, run by one Annabelle Thompson. At first I thought it was just a simple success story, your Southern California fad machine at work. But now I am not so sure.

---

[26] <http://www.cddc.vt.edu/journals/newriver/7/Fibonacci/choice.htm>

We are now launched into a mathematical, literary and visual multi-choice sequence in which every choice is a gamble and the 'reader' (we need a new word here) is invited to discover that numerical sequences combine with the computer to find order in chaos. One possible reading is that Fibonacci numbers represent facts of nature, forming a code that we see only in flashes – and that these perhaps echo the strange recurrences in the patterns of our lives and in the stories we report. It is only an illusion of fragile humanity that events have causes or consequences which we can control. If that *is* where the golden square is leading us (and presumably that depends on how many readings the user is prepared to engage in), then it is an interesting message and it is one that a story told between paper covers cannot tell in the same way.

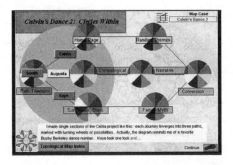

M D Coverley's more recent work *Califia* (2000) is a brave and ambitious work and the first I have come across that really tries to take the novel form into a new area, while also putting the quality of writing first. It is only online in sampler form[27], and on sale at Eastgate Systems. This is an innovative way of tracing five generations of Californians on a quest for a lost stash of gold. Its 'text' would run to about 300 pages of written words alone, thus needing the same attention from writer and publisher that a print novel would in researching, writing, rewriting and proofing. However, *Califia* is embedded in a structure of some 800 screens, 30 music clips and more than 2400 images, and this magnifies the work-load hugely. It isn't for the faint-hearted, as this extract about the process itself shows:

> While I did have a linear version of some of the text, I began the work with the whole concept in mind, so I was always operating within the larger

[27] <http://califia.hispeed/com/califia1.htm>

scope of the project. The tricky part was shaping the story to the constraints of the technology/media.

In a novel such as this, so many elements come into play, and all of them are inter-related. For example, about mid-stream, I decided to change the screen resolution. That meant changing the type faces, the navigation icons, the menus, the length of text on a screen, the size of the graphics, the position of elements on the page, the size of the pop-up windows, and so on. Or, securing credits for graphics and music.

I was lucky enough to have a garage-full of California artefacts and photos, but all of the music needed to be licensed. The Grateful Dead were gracious and helpful in getting me master copies of their music, and several local musicians donated their work to the project, but I spent the better part of a year securing the copyrights to the media that I wanted to use. And, in the cases where I could not afford the rights – another re-write.

Lest all of this sound discouraging, let me add that making *Califia* was one of the most exciting and rewarding activities I can imagine – the challenge of the medium, the delight in a totally new vocabulary of story-telling, the sensory pleasure of colour, sound, image, and structure; every day was a fresh adventure, a journey across the horizon of creative risk-taking.

This work is both linear and cross-linear and it illustrates just how adventurous and energetic new authors need to be. The audiences are currently small, but that has always been true of innovative art. It's also the case that most traditional novelists also have very small readerships – only a handful of well-known names at the top of the best-selling lists make a living. A Society of Authors survey of authors' earnings carried out in 2000 found that 75% of professional authors earned less than the national average wage. Digital literature has the advantage of being accessible to larger readerships and the material is accessible for longer, thus giving authors greater opportunities to benefit financially over a longer period.

If the reader wonders why I have chosen fictions that are much more than stories to illustrate this section, it is because I believe we need to be very inventive in our thinking about story-telling if we are to find ways in which they can break out of the beliefs of the traditional canon. Beliefs with which, in my heart, I agree – but also think innovative writing can, given time, overstep. Ian McEwan sums it up so well in the letter from a literary critic in his novel *Atonement*. Commenting on stream-of-consciousness writing, he has a fictive Cyril Connolly write:

The crystalline present moment is of course a worthy moment in itself, especially for poetry; it allows the writer to show his gifts, delve into the mysteries of perception, present a stylised version of thought processes, permit the vagaries and unpredictability of the private self to be explored and so on. Who can doubt the value of this experimentation? However, such writing can become precious when there is no sense of forward movement. Put the other way round, our attention would have been held even more effectively had there been an underlying pull of simple narrative.

Web story is still searching for this underlying pull. I do not think we should seek it in narrative, because we probably will not find it. But 'underlying pull' can be many things. In web environments it is likely to move through 'click-and-chase', but this is too passive a task, engaging only one hand and not the mind or the emotions. Story environments of the future will have to engage us more actively than that in order to challenge our ability to think and transform our emotional state.

Fantasy

Everyone in Wonderland

Entering into the imaginary worlds of virtual reality as part of the normal accoutrements of the home PC was at one time seen as the new way of engaging with the digital environment – but the headsets and eye-pieces required have not been forthcoming. Without those, true immersion in these alternative worlds does not occur; we are limited by the oblong space of the light box and all too aware of its boundaries.

The seeds for what we now call virtual reality were sown long ago in the poetic fantasies of Homer and came to a peak with Lewis Carroll's *Alice in Wonderland* (1865). Alice is drawn to follow a white rabbit on a fantasy adventure, reality is inverted, and the reader races with Alice down a rabbit-hole – suspending disbelief while all sorts of curious things happen on a bizarre underground journey.

The web has been involved in people metaphorically jumping down rabbit-holes ever since. At basic and more sophisticated levels are the writing spaces where people can invent themselves in a 'reality dissociated' environment. These are MUDs and MOOs and I have only a passing experience of them because they haven't held any appeal for me – in the early days of the web it was very complicated to join in with them and they did not hold my attention once I got there. MUD stands for Multi-User Dimension and it's a text-based virtual environment in which users from all over the world can interact in real-time. These virtual environments are often quite large and elaborate, comprising thousands of interlocked descriptions of various urban or countryside settings. Most are fantasy places and peopled by fantasy alter-egos who write to one another, at the same time constructing their own stories. MOOs (Mud, Object Oriented) provide a programming language that allows users to build their own additions to the landscape, creating rooms, furniture, coffee machines and avatar characters[28] which carry their alternative (wish-fulfillment fantasy) selves.

If you visit almost any Internet café you will see people deeply engrossed in one of the many websites that have developed from this concept. The café clientele are all writing fiction.

One website, Ultima Online[29], intrigued me because I once met a man who said he was going there on his two-week holiday and would spend all day everyday playing online. Like many other web games, it owes something to the dungeons and dragons narrative game-play (frequently embodied in MUDs and MOOs). It is a gothic world of science fiction, where people with that kind of imagination can explore their alter egos: the game theory relies on a system of avatars which permit individuals to choose different personae. It *is* a game, but a game with fictive dimensions offering a playroom for people to escape into online worlds. The writer of such fictions provides an environment, some rules and some seed ideas and then throws it open to the user to go and play. Here is a small flavour of this type of fantasy world:

> The target of a never-ending war of dominance, the facet of Felucca is home to the Ultima Online Faction system. Choose to align with the True Britannians, Shadowlords, Council of Mages, or the followers of the sorceress Minax, and join in the battle for control of the cities of the land. All of the rules and regulations of faction system combat can be found within – read on and join in this unique combat experience.

As the popularity of the Harry Potter and Tolkein books bear witness, magical worlds such as these have seemingly endless appeal. They work well in online fictions because they *are* rule-based and

---

[28] Graphical figures, as in videogames, with whom the user chooses to identify.
[29] <http://www.uo.com/>

therefore it is not an impossible task to script some likely behaviours of the person interacting with onscreen descriptions. But human nature is exceedingly complex and there is therefore wide-open opportunity for those writers who can capture more multifaceted satisfactions than those of troll-slaughter and adventure fantasy.

Glide[30] (2001) takes this genre a little further. It is an interactive exploration of visual language using a science fiction novel called *The Maze Game* by Diane Reed Slattery, who with her programming supporters has used animation, soundtracks and special effects in Macromedia Director – very sophisticated and professionally done. This is story-telling with a difference because there is an immersive story, but the user has to find out how to reach it. Part of the game involves downloading a lexicon to translate the 'glyphs' into English and a 'collabyrinth', which is an interactive space for communicating with and in Glide. Glide is a language in pictorial form, made up of triads of wave-like strokes (reminiscent of the triads in the *I Ching*). Part of the point of this is to explore why we are so hooked on logic as a means to story-telling, and whether there is a language of ambiguity that could be expressed by using a combination of media to advance the action. What meanings are there, asks the author, when syntax is on the move; when meaning derives from signs that don't form logical and sequential lines, but link into mazes or move about the screen?

This a difficult question to ask those of us for whom language is at the base of self-expression. It's possible that using language to describe or think about virtual spaces is in itself an obstacle to being able to understand and appreciate them.

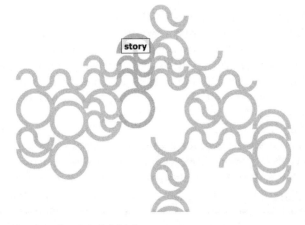

---

[30] <http://www.academy.rpi.edu/glide/>

There *is* a linear story woven into *Glide* about time-honoured themes such as life, death and immortality, but to read the story text by itself would be to miss the point. It opens thus:

> Dancemaster Wallenda of the Origin School of Death Dancers sat on a stone bench in the story circle at the centre of the maze, hearing his students approaching, his face buried in his hands. The voices of the children echoed – laughing, calling to each other – as if they were not at the end of childhood. They ran inward through the maze of glyphs. Wallenda had peeled off the thin strip of his eye-mask; it curled beside him on the bench, next to his scorecard. It wasn't a card at all but a small warm black ball, usually nestled in the centre of his palm. He needed his palms empty now, and his eyes uncovered. He needed to feel skin cupped over closed eyelids, that extra darkness. He needed his fingers free to stroke his temples. He could feel veins pulsing, even through the scars. There were minutes yet before they would arrive, plenty of time to press the mask back on.

Glide is a fascinating piece, not least because it was clearly extremely expensive to make. It's hard to see how the author and programmers are going to make any money out of it, as the full version seems to be openly available on the web to all-comers.

Avant pop

Beowulf, Andy Warhol and *Bled Text*

As I have said elsewhere in this book, I am *not* looking at deconstructuralist or post-modernist literary theories. I'd rather leave that to the critics and theorists. But I cannot ignore the wave of web artists whose work is founded in theoretical ideas and who regard themselves as being in a cultural vanguard. Wherever there is a democratic society, there are the current 'Andy Warhols' of it who are intent on developing their formal opposition to everything mainstream. *Horizon* magazine in 1947 said, 'A literature without an avant garde soon becomes a literature without a main body.' Warhol strikes one as someone who might have been drawn to the freedom of the Internet. He became a symbol of the 1950s and 1960s by appropriating and reinventing images from popular culture such as the Campbell's Soup Cans and a photograph of Marilyn Monroe from which derived the expression 'popism'.

The web has reinvented avant garde with its new coinage, avant pop – or, more correctly:

aVANT-pOP, sUR-fICTION, hYPER-fICTION

The phrase 'avant garde' dates back to Malory's *La Morte d'Arthur* in the 15th century (at least that is the earliest citation in the *Oxford English Dictionary*); 'avant pop' apparently dates back to a 1992 jazz album, so it carries a certain lusty freshness. Without wishing to attempt to categorise, or in any way suggest that such artists fall within a recognisable seam, it is possible to identify some characteristics of avant pop which include the following:

- visually loud, baffling or provocative front-entry points;
- a cavalier attitude to navigation convenience;
- self-referential themes that internalise the form;
- automated and animated routines that cut up words and sentences;
- an intermixing of personal neologisms, sprawling syntax, designer vocabularies and pseudo-genres;
- an appropriation of other texts and characters (though that has been changing as web avant pop 'grows up');
- serendipitous, on-the-fly readings operating through random interactions;
- attempts to bring verbal and visual sensuality into the writing-reading experience;
- fictionalisation of non-fictive themes;
- an unfolding over time;
- an incorporation of user feedback.

The avant popist experiences the web as a place of so much inter-connectivity that individuals need to redefine themselves in order to grasp hold of what that individuality is. It is both internal and multidimensional. This makes the artist both inward-looking (almost navel-gazing) while also reaching out beyond what they perceive as the current literary or language boundaries.

One of the founder members of the movement is Mark Amerika, who teaches digital art and theory at the University of Colorado at Boulder. His *Grammatron* (1997) was selected as one of the first works of Internet art to be exhibited in the Whitney Biennial Exhibition of American Art. The work grapples with the idea of spirituality in the electronic age, giving a machine-eye view of story-telling and story theory. Like many new media works, it blurs the boundaries between fact and fiction[31]. One of its opening screens (and any quotations can only give half the impact) states part of the avant pop mission:

> The cyborg-narrator, whose language investigations will create fluid narrative worlds for other cyborg-narrators to immerse themselves in, no longer has to feel bound by the self-contained artifact of book media. Instead of being held hostage by the page metaphor and its self-limiting texture as a landscape with distinct borders, Hypertextual Consciousness can now instantaneously link itself with a multitude of discourse networks where various lines of flight circulate and mediate the continued development of the collective-self as it rids us of this need to surrender our thinking to outmoded conceptions of rhetoric and authorship.

Avant pop at its most questioning forces readers to rethink what language and grammar is. Mary-anne Breeze – known as Mez – is an award-winning Australian writer/artist who has influenced much net art[32]. The quotation below is not so much part of a creative piece (since most of them demand moving screens) as it is 'writing on writing'. The first-time reader may resist the slowing down of comprehension that her form of iconoclasm takes. Those who have allowed themselves to pay attention, however, agree that the author does not play with language out of juvenility or trendiness, but with deliberate intent. Below is an example.

---

[31] <http://www.markamerika.com/>

[32] <http://beehive.temporalimage.com/content_apps34/app_c.html>

The Art of M[ez]ang.elle.ing: Constructing Polysemic & Neology Fic/Factions Online[33]

if:

pre alphanumeric//pre network n-cluded use ov com.put[ty/fillah]ers offline

then:

n-turr-rest in network system[ic]z stemmed fromme a more organic base, collaborationz were via real-time fleshmeat N n-stallation based

[d-tail n-hance.ment//philo.soph[omore]icall link wish n-sert:

movin amongst the pack[ette] ov life, we n-gage/ah-lert senzez that latah pull threads 2gether in2 a netwurked w.hole. x-samp.elle::when present-ting a papah on comp[lex]uter art in 93, the seed waz so[?]wn N x-periment.all edgez merged in2 the format of the aware, the concreted creatiff shift. all i hadde 2 do waz wait]

then:

the first html do[a]cumen.t _cutting spacez_ gestated in 1995, a hybridity year encased via a terminal discovered on the campus of wollongong university. many h[ertz]ourz spent chatting on Cybersite and Kajplats, channels dis[cobolos]coverin the er[k]rrorz N jo[uissance]y of this new textual realm. jumping fromme one terminal 2 the next//running three chat-roomz at once via three diffurrent terminal[behaviour]z sew as 2 opt.tim[id no lonah]ize the time d-layz, chairz blurring b-tween as the monitorz flashed fiction wurdz that [k]needed bleed.ed e.vent[ingz]ualli into the cutting spaces docco

[pause]

brief 4ray int MOOs; e.mail dependancee startz; transfer.all ov play became crucial here, while avatar patterns b-came e-vee-dent/m-merg-NT. di-wreck MOO based e.moti[vate]ng n-corporated in2 general fiction cre[che]ation. every.da[ze]ly chrono.logical time constricturez erased; temporal awarenezz irretrivably alt[.ctrl.delete]ered; geophysical statez became a hazy con[ned]struckt ov a "rl" [real life] parameter, with text no longah static and punct.ewe.ation actualizing in2 langue.

[d-tail n-hance.ment//physical link wish n-sert:

the computer became the real. terminal waz no longer a wurd 2 b feared, n-dicating abortive allusionz, but N actual object d-sign[n symbol]ed 2 n-hance, open, mutate. _my_ time became _mi_ own, mi text, mi fictional boundaries gellin with.in otherz azz yet known in a physical senze. blood N bone where no longah paramount outside of a textual wreck.cog[ging][ig]nition. B-ing parte ov the network opened up the fiction gatez N eye crossed ova in2 Bled Text.

[33] <http://netwurkerz.de/mez/datableed/complete/>

Bled Text is the author's own contribution to a view of language that she calls 'mezangelle' which allows linear language to go out of control and splinter into words and codes, and alter them in such a way as to extend and enhance meaning beyond the predicted or the expected. The significance of articulating codes side by side with words celebrates how much a part of our world electronic coding is.

Perhaps there is a liberation in this view of language. To what extent it is a new literary device is uncertain. Like many of the examples chosen to illustrate this chapter, it also harks back to an earlier era – to Beowulf and the oral poets who used the literary device called 'kenning' to help the listener visualise a spoken text. A kenning is a phrase used in place of a simple word. It consists of two words related to the object, but not necessarily to each other. Thus 'world-candle' stands for sun, 'gold-friend' for lord or 'whale-road' for sea. The kenning serves to slow down speech so that listeners can concentrate in a different way. In like manner, joining blocks of letters together in unusual relationships slows down the reader, allowing space or time for new thoughts and perceptions.

Mixed lexia

Pound and *Perplexia*

The juxtaposition of two elements without a conjunction has another device name, parataxis, and is characteristic of hypertext, coming into its vocabulary via oral poetry and modernists like T S Eliot in *The Wasteland* and Ezra Pound in *The Cantos*, which are structured around the juxtaposition of diverse fragments.

In discursive texts, writers tend to want readers to follow a logical sequence. So we use conjunctions, like 'so', 'however', 'but' and 'moreover' to move the flow on to the next block of thought. In web writing, one element does not need to follow another in a contained order. A click-link performs an act of jumping from one block to another. It is an action, not a conjunction; it turns readers into participants who make their own meanings.

These blocks are called 'lexia'. A lexia is a chunk of writing – a word, phrase, paragraph, chapter or article – that is linked to any or all of the others and is likely to be displayed in any order. The *Oxford English Dictionary* hasn't yet recognised it as a word, not even on its up-to-date website NODE, so let's try and get it in.

Roland Barthes used the term 'lexia' in the 1970s to denote 'units of reading' and more recently the critical theorist George Landow[34] defines it thus:

> Lexias are units of local stability in the general flux of the hypertext, invariant moments in the larger pattern of textual displacement. The relationship between the lexia and links that connect them is implicitly dialectical, a dynamic opposition of forces. The local stability of the lexia arouses expectations of coherence and internal consistency, familiar hallmarks of print; but the operation of the link overturns these expectations, constantly throwing the reader into unfamiliar discursive territory, invalidating apparent structures of causality and necessity. No wonder hypertext seems so problematic to researchers interested in coherence and unity: the experience of hypertextual reading is fundamentally dissonant.

In other words, a lexia is a chunk that links to another chunk; sometimes with no obvious linkage of meaning. It is up to the user-reader to find out, by moving the mouse around the screen, where the next related chunk is hiding itself. It becomes a guessing game to navigate between graphic elements and pop-up-and-vanish text units. It may require two or three readings before you understand anything at all and the idea seems to be that one approaches it like a game, rather than a linear story. To return to what I said about narrative above, the forward pull (if that is what it is) is that (as its author says) the 'interaction produces the narrative and the narrative itself is that of the user's engagement with the application'.

As with avant pop, playfulness with language is part of the slowing down process that forces the reader to pay attention. You need to be willing to go through the game of the several readings in the attempt to find meaning, and you probably need to overcome preconceptions from ways in which you have read before. It is impossible to give the flavour of this on the printed page, and if you wish to pursue it further you should certainly look at the most intelligent and also (intentionally) baffling example currently on the web: Talan Memmott's *Lexia to Perplexia*[35] (winner of the trAce/Alt-X new media writing awards in 2000). It's unfair on the work to quote, but we have already accepted that this chapter is

---

[34] Landow, George. Hypertext: *The Convergence of Contemporary Critical Theory and Technology*, Baltimore: John Hopkins UP, 1992

[35] <http://www.altx.com/ebr/ebr11/11mem/>

throwing out sparks that may intrigue readers to turn to the web and explore further, so below are some random sample lexia from the work.

(s) T (ex) T (s)

>> <<

*
—
*
—

[local.{[*...(*] |)}(...^...){(| [*)...*)]}.remote]

The self, already outside of the self, a first laquer of identity -- a screen or shell, a construct of how I imagine the body from the way I feel it -- locates (s)T(ex)T(s) a.part from it.self. As such, the self is already text -- showing ignitiative by appointing a(field) (in)Lieu. (of orgininal in)ten(t).ant to act on its behalf as the bracketed constructor of the original bi.narrative program.

The syntax of exe.change is based in the connection and collapse of announced and reserved constructs, and the conduction of [sub|ob]ject matter through these hybrids and mergers. Between the local and the remote, the success and failure of communification in the middle, the mess in the middle is prone to various mechanoid intensities borne from the simultaneous passage of others through the general conduit.

There are only ten screen pages in the work, but each page has many layers of lexia. The user has to unfold and unpack the screen, conscious always that the layers all overlap each other. It's not so much a case of 'reading' as of allowing oneself to 'infer' what is happening on the square of the screen. Clearly the writer enjoys the potential for complicating the dialogue about the differences between page and screen (as described in Chapter 1). Memmott's own commentary on the work in an online interview on the Alt-X site – 'where the digerati meet the literati' – elucidates, but only in part:

> The commentary within *Lexia to Perplexia* reflects heavily on the hidden narratives of our wanderings through cyberspace. As we transverse remote

regions of cyberspace from the comfort of our own terminals, a hidden formal narrative is written through our passage. This text, which is no doubt lengthy as we make deposits into various server logs, databases and pass through various protocols is in some ways transliterated through *Lexia to Perplexia*. The subject renders itself and the User becomes an unknowing protagonist in this missed.story. In regards to cyborganisation – of bodies with organs elsewhere – this is mostly developed through intent. Each cursor move marks a desire, of which we hope a specific object will be returned. This extra-mentalism, or hyperlobal operation is the most obvious form of cyborganisation, beyond the simple interfacing with a terminal. The extension of 'I' to include an elsewhere, even if that elsewhere is the terminal right in front of you (I+device), is how a Cell.f is initially constructed, and from it Cell.f ID.entity.

What Memmott appears to have introduced into the genre (he calls it 'rich.lit') is that writing words and writing code need not be kept apart. So he fuses HTML or JavaScript coding into the body of the message (a technique that other web artists are emulating).

There are many influences behind this type of work. One, lesser known than he should be, is B S Johnson, an innovative British poet, playwright, film and television director and journalist of the 1960s and 1970s. Here is another artist whom I think would have seen the potential of the web for breathing new life into literature. His works combine verbal inventiveness with typographical innovations. His *Albert Angelo* (1964) included carefully holed pages in order that readers might choose for themselves the order in which they received the writer's words. In it he says:

A page is an area on which I may place any signs I consider to communicate most nearly what I have to convey. Therefore I employ, within the pocket of my publisher and the patience of my printer, typographical techniques beyond the arbitrary and constricting limits of the conventional novel. To dismiss such techniques as gimmicks, or to refuse to take them seriously, is crassly to miss the point.

The phrase 'within the pocket of my publisher' is surely the key to the difference between the days of traditional publishing and now. It wasn't economic to play tricks with the book form, because it added costs and cut down the publisher's profit margin. Artists (as we see from the web now) have not been constrained in their own experimentation by economics, but to find backers for seemingly mad ideas has never been easy.

Johnson's novel *The Unfortunates* (1969) carried the pursuit of disintegration further – and here's a sad story which illustrates why web writers should be encouraged. The novel consists of 27 pamphlet sections contained in a box, which the reader can shuffle around and read in any order. The subject revolves round a journalist's day covering a football match in Nottingham, remembering previous times spent in the city with a lover now gone and a friend now dead. Throwing out the fixed page order and the linearity of the traditional book wasn't a gimmick, but a reflection of its subject matter – chaos, chance and memory. The book was a critical and commercial flop and the experience left Johnson deeply depressed. Four years later, he committed suicide. In 2001, Picador reissued the book in recognition that its time has now come.

Poetry

Emblem verse, concrete poetry and cyberpoetics

The web gives a new freedom to poets – and they have not been slow to recognise that animation and graphic design software has unleashed means of expression for which they have long been searching. Regrettably, it is not possible to show on the page any of the many ways in which digital poetry explores colour, variegated typefaces in animation, non-verbal typographical signs employed as text items, verbal or expressive sounds, and all manner of techniques for articulating words in movement. You must go to the web yourself and look. As good a starting place as any is UbuWeb[36] and I recommend searching for Christian Bök's *euonia, chapter e*, which simply cannot be reproduced on the page. What modern poets are doing in electronic space is exciting. New; yet not new.

It's unclear when the marriage between poetry and experimental typography began – even the ancient Greeks dabbled in figured poetry (i.e. a form resembling the subject matter). George Herbert, like the Elizabethan poets before him, was experimenting with patterned, or emblem verses, such as in 'Easter Wings' which is shaped like two wings (turned on their side) to symbolise the theme of the resurrection in the poem:

---

[36] <http://www.ubu.com/>

Lord, who createdst man in wealth and store,
Though foolishly he lost the same,
Decaying more and more
Till he became
Most poor:
With thee
O let me rise
As larks, harmoniously,
And sing this day thy victories
Then shall the fall further the flight in me.

My tender age in sorrow did begin;
And still with sicknesses shame
Thou didst so punish sin,
That I became
Most thin,
With thee
Let me combine
And feel this day's victory
For, if I imp my wing on thine,
Affliction shall advance the flight in me.

The mouse's tale (shaped like a tail) in *Alice in Wonderland* is perhaps the best-known example of a figured poem. According to *The Annotated Alice*, Carroll might have got the idea for this from a dream poem related to him by Tennyson. The poem, which was about fairies, started with very long lines and ended with lines of two syllables. Other poets famous for merging form and pattern with other poetic devices include Mallarmé, Marinetti and Apollinaire, and results are variously named as calligrammes, art chirography, parole in libertà, concrete poetry, and optophonetics. They have other names in Russia, Brazil, China and Japan where similar movements took place.

Using a diversity of word arrangements as a self-conscious activity probably flowered with the avant-garde post-war movements of Futurism, Expressionism and Dada which aimed (as does the web) to encompass all art forms. The aims were threefold:

- to use visual (or optic) devices;
- to use phonetics (or sound);
- to use kinetics (sequential movement).

All these are now easily done with web-design tools, and current experimental forms roughly parallel what the concrete poets were playing with. We now have hypertext, visual and kinetic text, and works in programmable media. In the 1950s and 1960s, only experienced typographers, performers or artists had the means at their disposal to express what their imagination could conceive, but then came letraset, photocopying and a range of self-publishing options that made it possible for anyone to explore concrete poetry. The computer opened this out, first with the dubiously artistic, but certainly ingenious, ASCII art, which used keyboard characters and the space bar to render all sorts of images – from little decorative additions on email signature sign-offs to fairly complex renderings of paintings. My thanks to Normand Viellieux for the rose on the right.

The paintings of ASCII art included re-enacting Botticelli's 'Birth of Venus' as a set of keyboard signs. This develops yet further in Talan Memmott's *The Berth of V.Ness*[37], whose opening screen is shown opposite – but it has to be experienced in its full Flash glory on the screen.

Visual poems powered by Flash challenge the reader, who now has to engage in a personal, reactive creativity. In other words, the reader must be willing to help create the poem. There is a different grammar at work in web poetry: without the willingness to rearrange expectations, the object which presents itself may seem baffling or inconsequential. Frequently, the text of a poem goes in

[37] <http://www.koreawebart.org/Talan_Memmott.html>

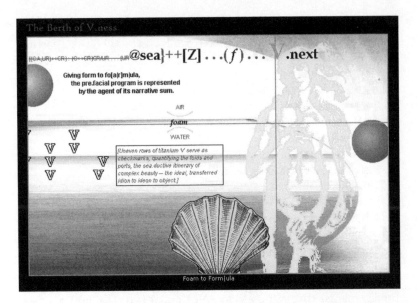

The Berth of V.ness

{(CA,UR}++CR} (O++CR)CR,UR ...UR@sea]++[Z] ...(ƒ) ... V.next

Giving form to fo[a]r]m]ula,
the pre.facial program is represented
by the agent of its narrative sum.

AIR

foam

WATER

[Uneven rows of titanium V serve as
checkmarks, quantifying the folds and
parts, the sea.ductive itinerary of
complex beauty — the ideal, transferred
idion to ideon to object.]

Foam to Form|ula

a loop of transformations on the screen, emerging and disappearing, evolving into shapes and patterns that express the meaning. The danger is that this visual and aural processing drains the poem of its meaning.

However, there is nothing new in that either. Take the poem 'bbbbetFmsbw' by Raoul Hausmann written in 1918 – a very 'webby' concept. Raoul Hausmann is one of the few Dada sound poets who made audio recordings of his sound poetry which are available online[38]. He had developed a system of notating phonetic poetry in 1918 which he called 'optophonetics'; this system used typographical variations to cue the manner of performance of the text. In an essay written in 1958 and available online, he writes:

> A poem for me is the rhythm of its sounds. So why have words? Poetry is produced by rhythmic sequences of consonants and diphthongs set against a counterpoint of associated vowels and it should be simultaneously phonetic and visual. Poetry is a fusion of dissonance and onomatopoeia. Poems emerge from the poet's inner vision and ear, materialising as the power of sound, noise and tonal form, anchored in the very act of language itself. Spiritual vision, spatial form and material sound form are not poetry in themselves but they all make up the poem.

---

[38] <http://www.ubu.com/feature/sound/feature_hausmann.html>

Optophonetic and phonetic poetry represent the first step towards poetry that is perfectly non-objective and abstract. Here's a section of Hausman:

```
K P'ERI UM L P'ERIOUM
N M' pernounnurn
bpretiberrerrebee onoooooooooh gplanpouk
kommpout perikoul
rreeeeeEEErreeeee A
oapderree ringlepadonou nntnou
tnournt
```

And below is a screenshot (randomly captured) of an animated work called *noth'rs* (1999) by John Cayley[39], who won the Electronic Literature Organisation's 2001 prize for poetry for the work *windsound*. Cayley described this work as a 'text movie' animated by transliteral morphs (textual morphing based on letter replacements) through a sequence of nodal texts. I could not find *windsound* on the web (nor a link to a sale venue), but his seemingly parallel work *noth'rs* plays through a sequence of partly composed and partly algorithmically generated sections of transliteral morphs based on Proust's *Du Coté de Chez Swann*, Jean Genet's *Miracle de la Ros*, Virginia Woolf's *To the Lighthouse* and Li Ruzhen's *Flowers in the Mirror*. The excerpt below needs to be seen in its context because the reader interacts with random phonemes and morphemes (as illustrated) and meaningful phrases and sentences in traditional poetic form.

```
i   i    i   i            a        i  t    i
I ad cajried i'inv initcit fa'l lhich  cottimv qy
its fpetd ind gelnoceyaty a'l tvreads tvat vold me
ti tvis rillt  fludves me into flamon  into foulness
into dreamidh ant gel'  enm fidally lidds pi in a i ti
vewdan of paimt'iness wjera ronep byood  lyses lgome    a
piauty    ib confosed oq the rimsiof thi fatays
tveil polds  vasjen  tops  sbots  inmtkt golis a  a
ploshes and eved nhear stepb jcixciali momsu witv
tho'ds                        i                a i
    t       t   i             i              i
     t         i       i  i                    i   i
         i             i              ai
```

39 <http://www.heelstone.com/meridian/cayley.html>

Experimental poetry is embedded within the history of the medium, and that is one of the reasons why the web has more to offer than do many of the other genres under discussion.

Interactivity in poetry is within a continuous tradition. Raymond Queneau is another web artist before his time: he was a member of a group called Oulipo, short for Ouvrier de la Littérature Potentielle, which also included Georges Perec, Italo Calvino, etc. In 1961, he published *Cent Mille Milliards de Poèmes*. He wrote ten different sonnets, and had them printed on strips of paper that could combine any of each sonnet's 14 lines with any 13 lines drawn from the others. Rather like booklets of mix-and-match heads, bodies and tails or landscape cards that are popular with children, one imagines. This makes up for an astounding number of combinations (10 to the power of 14). It is an interactive work before online resources made the process much easier. See how it is built online,[40] though the script is not maintained on the site and so it only partially works. Or view the randomiser[41] which also translates the French into English.

Visual poetry uses collage, text manipulation, colour overlays, blurring, fade-outs, rotation and other static or animation devices. It can be conceptual, concrete, calligraphic, emotional, minimal, mimetic and mad. It does not fit the 'usual' slots. Grouping keyboard character sets in quirky or original ways has its own, unconventional grammar. *Cloh!neing God N Ange-Lz*[42] by Mez (already mentioned for her *Bled Text* on pp. 70–72) won a JavaMuseum's Java Artist of the Year Award (2001) for its first Perspectives on New Media show. This cannot be read on paper, without its animations and visual additions. The piece explores the nature of contemporary cloning technology through a parody of quasi-religious animations. The work progresses through a series of biologically tinkered creatures, text and music that highlight the absurdities that cloning technology may produce, and the word animations both play with language and add layers to it.

Where do ideas such as these come from? Obviously there are many influences, but in my imagined gallery I would single out Kurt Schwitters, one of a generation of artists frowned on by the interwar regime of his day because his work was so subversive – clearly of the web-artist clan. His approach could almost be a watchword of online creativity: 'I prefer nonsense, but that is a purely personal approach. I feel sorry for nonsense because it has not been artistically moulded.' A lot of web artists now are seemingly sorry for nonsense – that is to say their work demonstrates that nonsense has a place in their hearts. Schwitters' work is rooted in collage, expressive of abstract drama and poetry, cabaret, typography, body painting, music, photography and architecture. We'd call it multimedia art now.

He established his own form of Dada, called Merz – a word fragment taken from a scrap of newspaper that he used as part of a collage in a random collection of waste objects. Though he is known mostly for his wit and humour in art, his credo was to demand absolute equality between words and pictures. As a book like this cannot show his work in pictorial form, the poem he wrote to Anna Blume in 1919 – which was slated by the critics – must suffice to illustrate Schwitters' turn of mind and show how he created a word collage cut from magazine clippings which becomes both a parody and a love poem at the same time. This poem is regarded by Merz aficionados as a classic, though it led to a rift between Schwitters and the central Dada movement. It invites comparison with several Internet poets.

AN ANNA BLUME
(*Kurt Schwitters' own translation* [43])
EVE BLOSSOM
Oh thou, beloved of my twenty-seven senses, I love thine! Thou thee thee thine, I thine, thou mine, we?
That (by the way) is beside the point!
Who art thou, uncounted woman, Thou art, art thou?
People say, thou werst,
Let them say, they don't know what they are talking about.
Thou wearest thine hat on thy feet, and wanderest on thine hands,
On thine hands thou wanderest
Hallo, thy red dress, sawn into white folds,
Red I love Eve Blossom, red I love thine,
Thou thee thee thine, I thine, thou mine, we?
That (by the way) belongs to the cold glow!
Eve Blossom, red Eve Blossom what do people say?
PRIZE QUESTION: 1. Eve Blossom is red,
2. Eve Blossom has wheels

[43] <http:www.soroptimist.de/eanna.htm> (by kind permission of DuMont Verlag, Cologne).

3. what colour are the wheels?
Blue is the colour of your yellow hair
Red is the whirl of your green wheels,
Thou simple maiden in everyday dress,
Thou small green animal,
I love thine!
Thou thee thee thine, I thine, thou mine, we?
That (by the way) belongs to the glowing brazier!
Eve Blossom,eve,
E – V – E,
E easy, V victory, E easy,
I trickle your name.
Your name drops like soft tallow.
Do you know it, Eve?
Do you already know it?
One can also read you from the back
And you, you most glorious of all,
You are from the back as from the front,
E-V-E.
Easy victory.
Tallow trickles to stroke over my back
Eve Blossom,
Thou drippy animal,
I
Love
Thine!
I love you!!!!

Letterplays – or words-as-letters, as distinct from words-as-phonemes or words-as-carriers-of-meaning – form the focus of much web poetry. I'll end this display with a form of word play called a lipogram, in which a particular letter of the alphabet is deliberately omitted from a piece of verse or prose – an esoteric writing exercise that has been practised for centuries in many different languages.

In 1939 an American named Ernest Vincent Wright composed a 50,000-word novel called *Gadsby* entirely written without the letter 'e'. Apparently, he tied down the bar for 'e' on his typewriter (you could do that in those days) so that he wouldn't accidentally use the letter. Thirty years later, in 1969, Georges Perec wrote the lipogrammatic novel *La Disparition*, best translated as *A Void*, which is also e-less. It is the story of the disappearance of a man; and in the world from where that man disappeared, the letter 'e' disappeared as well.

We now live in a society in which we are adding 'e' to everything: e-book, e-writing, e-publishers, e-poetry, e-commerce – e-nough!

Ross Eckler (who wrote a book called *Making the Alphabet Dance*[44]) took the nursery rhyme 'Mary Had a Little Lamb', and rewrote it in five different versions omitting various letters – the last of which removed half the letters from the alphabet and came up with this version, which uses only A, C, D, E, H, I, L, M, N, P, R, S, and T:

> Maria had a little sheep,
> As pale as rime its hair,
> And all the places Maria came
> The sheep did tail her there;
> In Maria's class it came at last,
> A sheep can't enter there;
> It made the children clap their hands
> A sheep in class, that's rare.

End of exhibition

This romp through literary influences concertinas centuries into a short space as exhibitions often do, with the intention of leaving the viewer a little breathless. I hope that this will be a creative breathlessness, with little sparks that shoot onwards. In my own creative work, I find that connections trigger ideas and scenarios. You, I hope, will build on from this 'room' of an – inevitably individual – choice of mixed media, adding genres from your own interests, such as epic, or satire, or miracle play, or romance, and their web parallels.

For those with a thirst for more, Part 3 has a listing of experimental artists and venues where multiple works can be found. Some have been mentioned above, but there are many more interesting pieces of work that did not find their way into this exhibition spread.

As for the interactivity of different reading choices, Dante used four levels when writing *The Divine Comedy* – literal, allegorical, moral and anagogical – and those modes would have been well understood in his day. So in what sense are we putting new lamps in the place of old? There is, of course, nothing new under the sun, but another way of looking at it is that new lamps give a different light.

---

[44] <http://www.wordways.com/>

4

Digital dimensions

The intention of the previous chapter was to show that creative flora breed in fields where others have been before. Those fields have been well cultivated, and it's a brave person who takes no account at all of the tried and tested husbandry methods of the past. It is exhilarating to rear new plant forms, but without water and sunlight they will not grow. Can we identify what must feed the roots of new-media art and fictions as we move into new digital spaces? All the advice for novelists, screen-writers and dramatists says that you cannot succeed without an interplay between structure, relationships and conflict. As the previous chapter showed, some web artists think you can. Some are looking at new ways of combining and working with these essential elements. And I say 'essential' because, like sunlight and water, these are what the reader craves.

But are we readers in quite the same way? Those who work in interactive games differentiate between 'lean-back' and 'lean-forward' activities. Lean-backers are people who read novels, short stories and comics, and watch films and TV: people who give themselves up to what unfolds before them. Lean-forwarders are those who bend in towards the screen, engage with it via a mouse or games joystick and control the action. They aren't readers or watchers; they are users or visitors.

In lean-back narratives, the action will not fundamentally change (although people have different readings of it that change how they personally interact with it, and what meanings they read into the action). In lean-forward narratives, the visitors do influence the action. Writers have to give up two elements that they have hither-to held in their power: choice and control. The visitor/user/player decides how to move through the narrative and how to control the way in which events unfold. Of course, that sense of control can be an illusion if the writer has a sufficiently tight grasp of a number of different outcomes and can manipulate the user into thinking that their choices affect the action.

Interactive productions still need an inner structural core. Reject the classic three-part construction at your peril: a beginning that engages the visitor with the situation; a middle that develops it; and a final section that unravels the end point. And if conflict is not the moving force, it's hard to see what will move the user onwards. Even the avant-garde online magazine *Wired* has article-writing guidelines that say, 'If there's no conflict – moral, institutional, cultural – there's no story.' Yet 21st century literary development has a belief in chaos theory, and holds that non-linearity in fiction can break the deterministic pattern of the 'conflict–crisis–resolution' model and still create a satisfying form.

This chapter looks at some of the different digital spaces that exist, what genres they support, and how they deal with interactivity.

Digital spaces

The browser window presents a space for text and image; always the same shape and size, like frame in an empty gallery. For writers this presents the complication that they are not writing on a surface, but writing into a space. These spaces come in various genre-defying forms of which these seem to be the favourites:

- multi-dimensional narrative;
- maps and urban space travelogs;
- installation/live performance;
- visual art/literature;
- game play;
- imaginary identity;
- essays in subversion;
- collaborative environments.

These spaces allow writer-artists to defy the boundaries and constraints of linear writing, visual art and computer programming.

Play space

Make-believe is as old as childhood and is a form of story-creation that is essential to healthy development. What's new in the computer world is that it becomes immersive in a number of seemingly contradictory ways. There's the solipsistic element: individuals play 'let's pretend' with themselves because the computer itself offers uninhibited access to emotions, thoughts, alter egos and places that are not available in real life. This contrasts with the role play that is enacted globally as people enact roles with each other (while being physically alone at home) and form deep relationships with others they have never met and who may not even be giving out real names or even their real sex.

Writers of interactive fiction can learn a great deal about structure from studying computer games, which have reached a high level of sophistication. I cannot claim to have explored the game world in as much detail as it deserves because it simply does not hold my attention. One interesting experiment was a CD of *Sophie's World* based on Jostein Gaarder's book which sold 12 million copies in 30 languages. This was produced in 1997 and comes closer than anything else I have seen to literary web fiction. The subject material was not mass-market, being the search for existential meaning.

There were 28 'scene-bands' that took the explorer through some of the history of human thought. To progress along the inherent linear strand required solutions to mensa-style puzzles. Help screens were cryptic: you had to find out for yourself how to make progress. This required a particular mind-set, not an ability to apply logical thought. The plot-ploy structure of the book gave way to point-and-click tricks to engage the reader, and the story (such as it is) proceeds via little emails floating across the screen plus communiqués between Sophie *et al* on a titchy palm-top. It was a brave attempt at an intelligent rendering of complex ideas. It must have been hugely expensive to produce: I doubt if it paid for its costs.

By contrast, at the end of 2001 the European Leisure Software Publishers Association found that UK sales of digital games reached an all-time high with sales just over 1.6 billion. The UK leisure software market is the third largest country market in the world, after the USA and Japan. In the UK, consumers now spend more on leisure software than on renting videos or cinema visits.

So there must be a potential market for the right story-game product. This book would be incomplete if it did not sketch in some of the areas in which interactive games can inform creative fiction writers.[45]

[45] For a deeper analysis, read Janet Murray's book *Hamlet on the Holodeck: The Future of Narrative in Cyberspace*, MIT Press, Mass. 1997.

Random adventure

In its most basic form, there is no story boarding, no site plan, just total randomness. An example of this is *Spiff*, an evolving interactive story that feels like a game, and it is growing all the time[46]. It is a random – and to me, not very satisfactory – process and is one version of what the web is doing to creative writing. The site explains itself:

> Welcome to *Spiff*. We have tried to create an experience that is different from most websites. For one, there is NO menu, NO navigation bar, and NO sense of where you are in the site. We did this for several reasons; one being that we will start at point A, and through a series of clicking on pages and choosing different routes, you will eventually get to point B.

> To truly experience *Spiff* you must slide your mouse over the entire page, scanning for links to different pages. All the links are not always obvious, so if you get lost, don't worry, there is a link somewhere on the page.

> Sometimes there are multiple links on a page that will take you to two completely different pages. If you keep following the links, you will eventually get to the end. There are also hidden pages and other fun stuff along your way.

Branching nodes

Branching structure (imagine a family tree) works like this: at chosen points in the game or story the player arrives at a decision point between various options – usually two; sometimes three. Those are the 'nodes' at which the action moves on. The story grows larger and larger as each path requires its own set of outcomes; it can loop back on itself as long as the story still makes sense. Branching points always lead back to a fixed number of nodes from where they branch out again. Without some control of the node points, you could have thousands of outcomes. In games, the node points are where the story-line develops. Writing a branching story is no easy task and the planning and scripting is 10–20 times the length of a standard story. All if/then possibilities must be covered even though some may never be chosen by the player, and to have satisfactory outcomes for each one is far from simple.

The narrative structure of many games is more rigid than it might look. Publishers do not want to spend money on expensive game content that the player may never get to experience, and so levels and

---

[46] <http://www.manipulation.com/spiff/>

tasks are used, which the player must complete in order to progress through the game. In this way, whichever choices players make in the course of the game, they will often find themselves in the same position further on. Writers cannot devise games on their own, but must join in teams. Their roles include: originating the initial game concept and putting together the proposal; writing the story of the game, or the 'game bible' for the designers to work to; writing the dramatised shorts that often occur between game levels; writing character dialogue; interactive scripting and interactive plotting.

The labyrinth or forking-paths effect is used in drama as well as in games and stories. Handled with care, this can lead to interesting results, but on the whole human relations are too complex and click-and-jump dramas can often become stories without narrative, with two-dimensional characters and a lack of emotional realism.

Parallel streaming

This is based on the 'like-life' premise that several lives are being lived at once, and the player can identify with one or more people and follow a story from their point of view (Virginia Woolf did this in *The Waves*). If you want to get into the minds or actions of another character, you have to start the game again. An example of this is given in the section on digital drama below (*see* page 96).

Story space

Story-tellers have used all sorts of media to entertain or educate audiences. Religious paintings frequently had a comic-strip element with several scenes from a saint's life represented in one composition. Song, dance, theatre, *belles lettres*, novels, film, radio, television and now the Internet all play their part in expanding the possibilities for story-telling. In live performances, the audience always has some effect on the way the story unfolds, even if the words have been written down or carefully planned beforehand. The stand-up comic bounces off people in the audience; the children's story-teller in a library can take a drama in one of a number of directions depending on the groundswell of reaction.

What is a story? How do you tell a story using general principles? *Are* there any general principles? How does the medium affect the way in which the story is told? Robert McKee has written a whole book running to 450 pages on the principles of story-telling in the genre of screenwriting, complete with diagrams of the 'spine of the story', where it relates to 'the inciting incident' and how most dramas progress through the classic three-act structure towards a resolution of an inner or outer conflict expressed earlier on. I simplify, but we are all familiar with the structure of a beginning act which propels you into the story, a middle act where events unfold, and a final act which moves towards an end-point.

In interactive stories, there is no such three-act progression. Insofar as it is relevant at all, the first act would be very brief – perhaps only a splash page offering different openings; the last act might also be very short, or it might diverge into a variety of multiple endings, or not be reached at all if the 'reader' went down too many blind alleys or made navigation mistakes. The second act (if we are using this structural idea) is actually the bulk of an interactive story moving backwards and forwards in time and space at will. The 'second act' occupies the digital story space and celebrates unpredictability. In my own original concept for this book, I had planned to write the web version of Robert McKee's book. Where he subtitles his book, 'substance, structure, style and the principles of screenwriting', mine was to offer the same for web writing. It rapidly became obvious to me that digital story spaces all had their own dynamic; the idea of 'substance, structure, style and principles' cannot be sustained.

Web writers have radically divergent assumptions about what stories can do as they move from print into an electronic environment. Most consider plotted narratives as wholly inappropriate for expression within this new medium, but while recognising that new options will replace traditional narrative, there is little agreement about what those options should be.

As all the examples in my imaginary exhibition show, web writers play with the relationship between author, reader and writer, with intent to baffle – not to lead with the kind of omniscient authority we are used to from conventional fictions. Instead, they upturn the core issues of the medium: the role of narration and story within the electronic medium; ways in which identification with character can occur (through multiple starting-point choices); and the need to invent formal conventions (including those producing more radical forms of reader interactivity than merely selecting which links to follow) which electronic fiction will need if it is to continue evolving into the major literary form it intends to become.

The trouble is that web writers throw out narrative at their peril because, as Phillip Pullman said in a BBC interview, 'If there is a tussle between intellectual concept and story, then the story should always win.' In story spaces on the web, the prime idea wins.

Puzzle space

Allied to play spaces are those with puzzle appeal. When Steven Spielberg's film *A.I. Artificial Intelligence* was released in 2001, the advertisers dreamed up an elaborate promotion. More than 30 websites popped up, apparently related to the death of one Evan Chan, and introducing a growing cast of personalities and bits of a complicated plot, all fictitious.

The elaboration develops out of a web search. It starts with a cryptic detail in the movie trailer's credits, where the name 'Jeanine Salla' is sandwiched between the names of the costume designer and composer John Williams. She is credited as a 'sentient machine therapist'. Entering the name Jeanine Salla into a search engine turns up several subtly fabricated sites, such as 'Bangalore World University', where Jeanine Salla is listed as a faculty member:

> Salla began her research career as a graduate student under Allen Hobby during his last years at the Aragon Institute of Technology.

To advance the story and gather more information about the so-called murder, gamers have to solve a series of increasingly difficult puzzles, by scouring the phoney sites for clues, searching for related characters and factoids, even responding to faxes, emails and phone calls from characters in the game. The fabrication is amazingly complex. You can explore the *A.I.* hoax and all of its sites, clues and diversions, through the semi-official Cloudmakers 'fan' site[47]: it is worth some investigation because it is clear that large numbers of people are hooked on puzzle-play like this, and it may give new writers further clues about what will appeal in web fictions.

Installations

All art forms are moving towards a blurring of the boundaries that traditionally exist between each discipline. Living sculpture, for example, fascinates because there is something that plays with expectations in watching living people make themselves into inanimate objects. Also, we ask the question, 'How do they do it?' The answer to, 'Why?' is that this is a form of installation in which the audience is reanimated. The web offers an exciting new space for installations – one which could be explored much further than it has so far.

[47] <http://www.cloudmakers.org/>

The art world has for several years now embraced art installations as well as traditional painting and sculpture, but writers have been very slow to take up the idea of writing as installation. Will Self did it by sitting keyboarding in the fig-1 Gallery in London (June 2000), writing people who came into the gallery to view him into a word-processed piece that was flashed up on a large screen behind him. Audience became both voyeur and participant and this was later widened out to the wider audience of a newspaper column (printed in *The Independent*).

It's worth mentioning the Turner Prize, sometimes also known as the Prize for the Emperor's New Clothes, at this point. This is a London art prize given to artists' installations and is frequently met with incredulity and outrage on the part of some contrasted with deep philosophising on the part of others. Typically contested winners include Chris Offili's elephant dung paintings, Tracey Emin's soiled bed and dirty knickers and Damien Hirst's sliced and pickled animals.

Martin Creed won the 2001 prize for 'an empty room with lights that flicker on and off every five seconds'. (Previous works include a scrunched-up piece of paper, a ball of Plasticine stuck to a wall, and several neon signs bearing messages such as The Whole World + The Work The Whole World and Everything Is Going To Be All Right.) The curator of the Tate Gallery commented, 'The fact that many people find his work so baffling indicates that he's working on the edge.' The artist himself warned that people should not look for too much meaning in his *Work 227: The lights going on and off.*

What's interesting in a web-writing context is Creed's own comment on his work: 'My work is about 50% of what I make of it and 50% of what people make of it. Meanings are made in people's heads. I can't control them.' The room in which the lights went on and off is just a large space where others can use their imagination by responding to what the space suggests.

In like fashion, the web offers spaces where writers too can present an offering and hope that others will match their initial idea with further work of their own. Three examples of writing as installation are given below.

1. *My Life in a Bag* by Robert Richardson (1999)[48] is an installation (now viewable as an online photograph) which consists of notes written by the artist to himself most nights over a ten-year

---

[48] <http://www.axisartists.org.uk/all/ref6605.htm>

period, as a reminder of the next day's tasks, meetings, and so on. These notes are spilling out of the canvas bag in which they have been kept and act as a self-portrait or document of a life.

2. *Foreign Logics*, an installation by writer Bernard Cohen and artist David Bickerstaff[49], presents 30 tourist episodes in a prose work conceptualised for screen-based, interactive reading. Its texts appear as chance encounters, unexplained interruptions to a journey, and places where words seem to drift in and out of meaning. It offers the tourist's experience of language: mistranslations, words overheard and partly comprehended, language used too fast or stretched out so slowly that the beginning of a sentence disappears as its end approaches. The installation appeared at the Bath Literature Festival (2001) and then toured before being released as a saleable CD-ROM in 2002 (after this book was written).

3. London-based Book Works[50] is sponsoring some interesting text-related projects in the form of exhibitions, installations, time-based and performance works to promote books videos, CD-ROMs, and new-media web projects. For example, *Reading Karl Marx* is an ongoing investigation into the act of reading as an artistic and pedagogical activity. This online project is a dedicated site, documenting the various reading seminars that he has carried out internationally. These seminars themselves are supplemented by an online community where visitors offer reactions.

I find the concept of writing combined with installation very exciting and am sure it can develop as it has done in the art world. Economics possibly work against this until such a time as some Saatchi-equivalents place a value on writing art.

Mobile phone space

Mobile phones could one day serve as a story-telling medium. I belonged at one time to a group of authors who were exploring text messages as a means of telling serial stories to subscribers; a short extract would be delivered every day for readers to enjoy on their daily commute. The constraints of the tiny screen would force writers to present material in a concise and effective manner. We

[49] <http:www.da2.org.uk>

[50] <http://www.bookworks-uk.ltd.uk/>

were experimenting with self-portrait narratives of 160 characters each (that being the limit of WAP phones at the time).

We were also interested in the idea of nationwide performance by mobile phone. One proposal suggested that every week, at the same time, a message would be sent out giving a simple action to perform. The action would be randomly chosen from a database which the mobile phone-in public could add to. Another idea was for theatrical ghost walks or treasure hunts, with instructions to destinations given via SMS with commentaries, ghostly sounds and events delivered aurally at the designated spots.

SMS stands for Short Message (or Messaging) Service and is the texting system that enables mobile phone users to send and receive text messages. Abbreviations allow maximum use of limited space. SMS is quick to write and can be a source of entertainment to both sender and receiver.

The cellular structure of the mobile network could also function like nodes in a branching narrative structure. On entering a physical network cell, the reader can be sent a text message that has some relevance to their surroundings. A physical object (building, road, billboard, river, etc.) might act as a visual cue. Each message gives part of the overall structure of the narrative space, so the reader's experience is one of detection, piecing together each fact or memory of one person's life. The ultimate goal could be to understand the disparate clues and so identify a physical location. At this location something real and physical might happen.

Laura Watts, a creative writer with a background in telecommunications, was commissioned to produce a script for a trial version of a mobile-phone-based interactive story. She notes that the development of the script was a demanding experience:

> The key issue for me was to provide a scenario which integrated the mobile phone, as a personal artefact, with a personal narrative. I was also keen to create a real-time experience so the story ran over a fixed number of days, giving it a sense of simulated reality. As with all interactivity the script needed to balance the potentially exponential increase in possible choices against the reader's sense of autonomy. Being a real-time story it had the added consideration of making acceptable demands on the participant's time whilst maintaining a sense of involvement.
>
> All these issues required substantial user testing, which the trial was designed to address. Mobile phones also have very specific and limited modes of interaction, and it was important to use these appropriately. Short messaging is suitable for some aspects of the narrative, voice mail and

WAP or Web pages for others. Having been a professional mobile phone interaction designer I was familiar with many of the interface issues; however, it was still a challenge to create a ten-day script. While this particular project did not go beyond trial, it did highlight to me some of the particular problems regarding the integration of fictional narratives with convergent media devices in relation to their social roles.

The story unfolded the layers of conspiracy and plot surrounding a company researching human genetics, and a mysterious organisation in its shadows. The participant was to take the role of the lead character's conscience, using their mobile phone to hear recordings of the character's findings, decisions and fears. As the plot developed and the character's conscience became manipulated by events, the participant had to choose a path between belief, fact and fiction.

Mobile phone narratives such as this are still at a pre-testing stage and will require much development. There remain very few examples of stories that attempt to involve a participant in a complex narrative using such an apparently limited medium. The creative challenge is to explode our preconceptions of the traditional role of mobile phones whilst acknowledging their technological constraints.

Communication technologies have already been brought into play in a project called 'silophone'[51] physically located in a silo in Montreal. Silophone collected sounds from around the world using mobile and Internet communication technologies and fed them into a physical space 'to create an instrument which blurs the boundaries between music, architecture and net art'. Sounds were transformed, reverberated, and coloured by the echoing acoustics of the structure. This sound is captured by microphones and rebroadcast back to its sender, to other listeners and to a sound installation outside the building. Anyone could contribute material of their own, filling the instrument with increasingly varied sounds.

Among the installation ideas in the group I belonged to were:

- A bronze talking head that speaks text message lines which have been sent by mobile phones.
- A fountain with a jet that could go into one of two different receptacles, so that a small movement of the jet can make the entire pattern of the fountain change. The jet would move left or right according to votes placed through WAP.

51 <http://www/silophone.net>

- A theatre performance where, in addition to the actors, there's a puppet with limited movements on stage, controlled in real time by phone-wielding members of the audience. (I have experienced something a little similar at the Institute of Contemporary Arts in London, where mobile-phone owners sent text messages about their perception of what was occurring onstage to a screen behind the performers. We, the audience, were eavesdropping on other audience members' comments on the performers of which they themselves were unaware. It was a curious sensation, possibly with some performance potential.)

We were a geographically disparate group and none of our ideas took off. But I think it worth throwing the idea of location and place in mobile communication and relationships into the pot. I do foresee a future for it as a new artistic space – a writing medium for creative and emotive installations.

Digital drama

Interactivity has always existed in drama, from Greek oralcy onwards. Dramatists and broadcasters make use of interactivity to gain emotional responses – they make their audiences laugh or cry (some, as in the Jerry Springer show, make them fight). Audiences used to write in with comments and complaints; now phone-in programmes invite interaction, and phone voting can change story outcomes – as can public outcry affect the story line of soaps such as *The Archers* (even Conan Doyle had to bring Holmes back from death at the Reichenbach Falls as a result of public dismay). Some ways in which dramatists are looking at interactive opportunities are discussed below.

Multi-view dramas

Like the interactive features of certain televised sports, the user can operate a player-cam, and watch the drama unfold from the perspective of different characters. For example, Alan Ayckbourne wrote three plays called *The Norman Conquest Trilogy*. The plays, which are meant to be seen in sequence on three successive nights, tell the same story from three different points of view, with various entrances and exits that link the three plays to one another. A BBC video production of this drama created an environment where the user could play the three pieces and flit between them at will. As each piece played, characters would become tinted either grey or green. A grey tint on the character signified that clicking on them would show a flashback to a previous scene in the play. A green tint would signify a flash forward to a related scene in the future. While the character was tinted, the phrase that was causing the memory, or glimpse into the future, was displayed below the video.

Web drama

I have already mentioned *Online Caroline* (*see* page 57) in the context of its relationship to the epistolary novel, but it also comes into this section. Ingenious though it is, *Online Caroline* is essentially a branching-plot story with a linear episodic narrative varied by the use of personalised elements. You think you are interacting because the way in which you react determines the way the story is told. As some of the narrative is video, some audio, some to be read onscreen and some appears in your email, you think it is tailored to you – whereas in fact, you are being influenced by keywords you gave earlier.

Cross-platform genre

Big Brother is an example of a manipulated story told across platforms and using actors from real life. Its success was not just the result of the dubious pleasure of voyeurism, but also because television, the web, phone voting and text messaging were all used simultaneously to enhance the drama. This allowed audiences to explore the 'back story' to such narrative as there was, including delving into expert psychological insights, and to make some contribution to how the drama unfolded as viewers decided who should be evicted from the house.

A web version of this idea is the interactive comedy *It's Your Dinner Party*[52] – an interactive drama based on regular dinner parties and devised as a game of consequences. Choose the guests, the seating plan and the menu and then sit back for ten-minute episodes of video-streaming on a minute window to witness the guests in personality clashes, skirmishes, flirtations and seductions. Then vote for your favourite seven guests and see how episode six (the last one) changes according to your choices. You think you are altering the

[52] <http://www.dinnerparty.tv/>

outcome, but obviously the creators have programmed-in a number of possible outcomes. There are a few nice touches, though: you can download the recipes of the dishes the guests are eating and watch the chefs in action. It's got the relationship and conflict interest that some web fictions deem unnecessary.

To give you a flavour of its *Big Brother*-type profiling, meet Billy:

> Despite what some people might see as rather a lonely lifestyle, Billy refuses to allow people to feel sorry for him for long. He has a naïve enjoyment of life's little pleasures, which probably comes from having experienced very few of life's greater ones. He throws himself into his job as a supermarket internal affairs supervisor with gusto, making it his business to be fully informed of the private lives of all his subordinates and offering help and guidance when and where it is needed.

All the guests are profiled and filmed, creating enough 'back story' on which to build a plot that is driven by character rather than situation. This site is heavily sponsored by advertising – obtrusively so – and is a very early 'flicker' stage of the medium. The video-streaming is very grainy and plot lines not startlingly inventive, but it has some elements worth following through to show how the genre could successfully develop when the technology delivers what it requires. The likelihood, though, is that we will get yet more sophisticated and require even better technologies as the current barriers are reached.

Audio streaming

The first UK interactive radio play was broadcast on Radios 3 and 4 in September 2001. It went out on two consecutive nights to give multiple story opportunity. Radios 1 and 2 declined to join so the third stream was only available synchronously on the Internet. There were three plays, written by Nick Fisher (he called them 'configurations'). The listeners were invited to create their own play by choosing one of the three characters. On cue, at intervals of about a minute, the listener then had to twiddle the tuning knob (if they didn't have digital radios) and follow another character on the other channel.

This is much easier on the web, where the 'plays' now reside on the BBC website[53], though only viable for those on unmetered con-

---

[53] <http://www.bbc.co.uk/radio4/wheel/>

nections because the audio streaming is slow and the buffering is clunky. One play is called *Transmission Control Penhaligon & The Thirty-Three Banana Problem*; the second is *The Probable Professor and His Uncertain God*; and the third is *Dawn Gambler – Long Night – Evening Odds*. Each focuses on a different character who switches into any other character's worlds. In an e-zine interview in Eastgate's online e-zine *Hypertext Now*, Nick Fisher says:

The very beginning of the writing process on *The Wheel of Fortune* – settling on my theme of chance and probability – was just the same as on any other project. But thereafter everything was different. And nothing was normal.

Developing the plot (or rather plots) required not just linear work as usual but a constant cross-referencing. And once I started writing, I knew I had to continue in non-linear mode. Consequently I wrote the first minute or so of Steve's story, then Leonard's, then T's. Then the next minute of each, etc. I continued this process of banding throughout. A totally new experience for me.

I spent a lot of time on what I call the junctions – the points at which the audience is invited to change from one configuration (the traditional idea of a play doesn't seem appropriate) to another. Sometimes these junctions provide moments of dislocation. At others sentences hang in mid-phrase – to be picked up in three totally different but grammatically correct ways on the three separate streams. Sometimes a segment ends with a question – which will be answered in different ways. And of course those answers are to three completely different queries.

To give an example may help explain what I mean. At one point the physicist, Leonard, is pondering the two worlds that surround us – the visible and the invisible. And he asks, 'What controls both?' At this point the listener can go three different ways, and get three different answers to Leonard's question:

'God.'
'Random Access.'
'Roulette.'

One may also arrive at these three answers from two other starting points. In one, a character is left in mid-sentence: 'This is the first time I've tried....' ('God...Random Access...Roulette') In the other, someone is pondering the uniqueness of things with a phrase that crops up several times in the course of the action and therefore makes more sense in context: 'What makes each have its own, wholly individual series of ifs and buts and maybes?' ('God...Random Access...Roulette')

The comments on the BBC web-board, where listeners have their say, were not overly enthusiastic. But what's interesting for writers who develop interactive broadcasting further is to learn from the processes. Fisher believes that artists must explore any and all new possibilities for expression, not with a view to novelty for its own sake, but to learn what it can tell us about creativity. Perhaps you can only learn by doing it yourself.

Immersion

An intriguing wave in web dramas is to blur the lines between fact and fiction. 'You only use 12% of your brain. Mind if we play with the rest?' ask the creators of the game Majestic[54]. And Electronic Arts, who created the site, explain:

> Majestic is an episodic online entertainment experience set against the back-drop of a grand and sinister conspiracy – an unfolding mystery adventure that uses the Internet as a canvas for its story, weaving you through both real and fictional experiences in real time. Highly personalised and natural-ly paced, Majestic tailors your experience specifically to you as it dynamically changes the content of web pages, emails, faxes, voice mails and chat con-versations in order to immerse each player at the very heart of a developing story. Majestic players assume the leading role in their own adventure, inter-acting with other characters, uncovering clues, searching for answers, collecting and using digital objects and resolving challenges to progress through the experience. Unlike other forms of entertainment, Majestic actively pursues and interacts with you based on events developing within the fiction, creating a uniquely suspenseful entertainment experience.

The game was a suspense thriller that infiltrated your life via the web, phone and fax. Tony Feldman, an expert in virtual environ-ments, comments:

> The intriguing question about Majestic is whether it is just another computer game, one that has found an especially striking way of engaging players and driving word-of-mouth hype, or whether it represents a genuinely new para-digm for interactive entertainment. The answer is that it is a new model, but one based on an old and eternal verity about all entertainment media. Electronic Arts has been smart enough to focus on the abiding truth that enduring success in on- or offline entertainment depends not on the fireworks

---

[54] <http://www.majesticthegame.com>

of its delivery, but on capturing hearts and minds – and doing this by engaging the myriad individual imaginations of the folk who constitute big audiences. Each person is unique, so personalised interactivity is important to respond to their individuality. But more important is the use by the game of so many of the prosaic channels of everyday existence so that the entertainment experience seeps through all of life's pores. This is bold and new. Getting phone messages from Majestic characters who say they will call you tomorrow and then do so, or receiving faxes from unknown sources who know more about you than they should, will make players nervous enough to start fearing an unexpected knock on their front door in the middle of the night.

It's worth pointing out that writers and players alike need serious technology to engage in a drama like this. For Majestic, you needed:

Windows 95, 98 or Me
166 MHz Pentium
32 Mb RAM
3 Mb hard drive space
4 Mb video card
Minimum 56K Internet connection
Flash 4
RealPlayer 8
AOL Instant Messenger 3 or AOL 5
IE 4.01, Netscape 4.75
    or AOL 5 (Majestic does not support IE 6 or Netscape 6.x)
HTML-capable email reader
Download size: 9 Mb
Time: 38 min. with a 56K modem

Interestingly, the game was a critical success, but within six months the producers decided to take it offline because it was not popular with players. They are now focusing resources on 'new, more popular content'. One can only wonder what that might be and what that means for the future of this medium. When I wrote this chapter, Majestic was just new and seemed to signal a new development that writers could benefit from. By the time I came to edit this chapter, the producers had announced that they were drawing the game to a close. Authors interested in this field should watch to see what Electronic Arts come up with next as they have clearly learnt from this hugely costly exercise. It's possible that this type of immersion is not what the general public is looking for.

Digital writing for children

The web is bound to promote many opportunities for children's writers simply because we are now such a picture-led society. Understanding what pictures say and what they mean is as important as understanding a train of logical thought. In previous generations the word 'illustration' meant to 'show something again', to pick out something that the text described. Today the pictorial representation is far more likely to be in the centre of a page and the explanatory words will 'illustrate' the illustration.

In addition, writing is becoming more image-like. Writing is frequently tailored to fit into a screen. Such layout favours bullet points and other graphic ways of arranging texts in short chunks for easy reading. Screens are not organised by the logic of writing, but by the logic of image. There is a change in mood of reading – the eyes move web-wise around pages rather than from left to right.

This is a huge culture shift. It presents a new communication landscape in which learning how to deal with digital images is paramount. Writers can draw out children's visual literacy by exploring the different narratives of image, animation and photography.

Screens are increasingly the site of all information and have been for the whole of the last century – with computer screens overtaking film screens. Children are comfortable with small consoles and with manipulating tiny screens similar to digital camera screens.

Image is more precise than language in some circumstances. It offers clear-cut realisations of faces, features, landscapes and so on. By contrast, children reading stories will fill in the vagueness of language with pictures from their own imagination.

One example of an interesting use of pictures as coded information was the heavily illustrated children's book *Masquerade* written and illustrated by Kit Williams (1979), which anticipates the web with its inter-mix of fiction and reality. It tells the story of the Moon falling in love with the Sun who calls on the help of a hare to deliver a fabulous jewel as a token of his affection. Hidden within the story is a master riddle which, when solved, directs the reader to the exact spot where a real 22-carat gold hare is buried somewhere in the British Isles. This had quite a cult following for a short time, and the hunt lasted for two years before two readers unpicked an ingenious code in the colour used in the pictures to find the hare under a stone cross in Bedfordshire.

The web has been relatively slow to wake up to the new possibilities of web literature for children. It has tended to concentrate on educational resources rather than innovation, and there are *quantities* of websites falling into this band. The web also encourages children's own story-writing – children writing for children and writing collaboratively. KidPub[55] is an example of the type and quality of writing on sites of this kind, and its particular value is in giving children an opportunity to have their work displayed and read. Interestingly, writing by and for children on the web has kept along fairly traditional lines: children like being told stories.

Devices

There are no rules in creative web stories, but there are some themes which seem to crop up repeatedly (just as drama uses plot ploys such as overheard conversations, items such as dropped handkerchiefs, and so on). One day someone will write a whole book on devices that work well for interactive spaces. At the moment, however, everyone is learning by observing what others are doing. For those just beginning or uncertain how to work with the genre, it may be useful to have a few jumping-off points. The ideas below come from a variety of sources and suggest that students new to digital spaces might want to work within one of the following forms, writing a set of 15–30 discrete word chunks (or lexia – *see* also page 72) to express a moving narrative or dramatic situation:

- a labyrinth with forking paths;
- a journey;
- a visit to a simulated place;
- the map as metaphor (e.g. maps of the body);
- a dictionary or encyclopaedia.

You could then map out three different paths through the narrative (with different outcomes) and use three or more of the following devices:

- progressive digression (as in *Tristram Shandy*);
- spatial schema (map, floorplan, labyrinth);
- single or multiple chronological schema (clock, calendar);
- multiple points of view on a single event;
- deconstruction of the form;
- hot-word linking (hypertext);

---

[55] <http://www.kidpub.org/kidpub/>

- nested stories;
- expanded footnotes (like Nicholson Baker's experimental novel *Mezzanine*, which consists largely of footnotes on a single lunch-hour in which the action centres on the protagonist drinking a milkshake and tying his shoelace).

Alternatively, you could set up a sequence of short paragraphs to fit into a game scenario of the following type:

- alien – predator – situation – fear;
- action – frustration – adventure;
- detective – conspiracy – solution;
- journey – obstacles – treasure.

As you progress into the narrative, you can either explore laterally along a horizontal axis, or delve down, burrowing further into layers of meaning. Whether you decide to have an outcome or a conclusion is a matter of choice, but the classic device of the three-act structure still takes a lot of beating. This has a beginning which propels readers into the action; a middle where events complicate or unfold; and an end-point which is where the whole thing is aiming. In interactive stories, the middle section is the one that requires the most writerly skill in creating a fictional universe. The beginning can be quite brief, with little interaction, and the end – if there are dead ends or multiple endings – may never be reached at all.

Principles

From the above, it looks as if works that appear in digital spaces might be based on some or all of the following principles:

- **Continuity**: writers can create worlds with their own logic, peculiarities and sensibilities – even their own languages; and visitors can browse, explore and make their own discoveries within the space.
- **Control**: even if the interaction is limited or illusionary, the viewer should have strong feelings of ownership over what unfolds and be involved in a much closer manner than traditional narrative allows.
- **Community**: digital spaces often work best when supported by chatrooms where visitors can meet and interact with other viewers.

But as the technological requirements above suggest, none of this is for the faint-hearted and engaging in digital narrative, drama or poetry is outside the range of the lone writer scribbling in a garret (poetry being partially excepted). You'll need collaboration teams.

There are perhaps nine problems and nine opportunities with interactive story-telling[56], and these are discussed below.

Problems

1. *Complexity*: full-length works are often difficult and require considerable collaboration, at technical, creative and business levels. Making a story work all the time on all platforms, with a number of partners (all expecting some income), is an enormous production challenge.
2. *Ignorance*: publishers do not know much about interactivity and don't see the need for exploring new types of narrative or drama.
3. *Bad tools*: interactive dramas are produced in a multi-platform world, in which hardware, software, middleware and operating systems can all have compatibility problems.
4. *Bad business models*: how do you make money from interactive content? There are numerous ideas, from micro-billing to sponsorship, but no established model.
5. *Big media prejudice*: while the large media companies are happy to exploit tried and tested genres and products, convincing them to experiment and innovate is difficult.
6. *Audience apathy*: large parts of the audience are not interested in interaction, and are content with the standard, passive entertainment forms.
7. *Good alternatives*: there is a great deal of competition for both the audience and talented writers, from books, film and other traditional forms of story-telling.
8. *Timescale*: how long can we wait for a mass-market Internet and broadband uptake? Many necessary developments are simply taking too long for interactive drama to get going.
9. *Closure*: there are some social questions about the nature of authorship and audience. For example, what are the reader expectations about updating published work? Has an author ever really 'finished' a work in a world of electronic distribution and user feedback?

---

[56] I am indebted to Tim Wright, who gave a seminar for New Media Knowledge, for the numbered points. I have expanded these from his original listing, which had its basis in drama.

Opportunities

1. *Collaborative*: through interaction and co-authorship, writers can create many more personal experiences for web visitors.
2. *Open-ended*: unlike traditional dramatic situations, there is no need for a Big Ending. There are opportunities for creating a mixture of platforms, characters and locations to develop rich, continuous experiences.
3. *Playing with reality*: with interactive stories, fact and fiction can be blurred in new ways to provoke interesting responses and questions – what's real and what's not? Where and when does the drama end?
4. *Fluidity*: interactive stories are less constrained by usual dramatic conventions. Writers can create fluid narratives with their own logic, rules and eccentricities.
5. *Spatial movement*: the user's journey through the narrative allows for architecture to become narrative, with space used to help tell the story, rather than just time.
6. *Role-play*: interactive stories allow for creative role-play and the fabrication, switching and merging of identities on the behalf of the audience and creators.
7. *Connectivity*: unlike passive forms of entertainment, online fictions can create social spaces and connect people together in creative and interesting ways.
8. *Personalisation*: interactive stories can be experienced directly by the end-user, in ways that are unmediated by broadcasters, brands and publishers.
9. *Immersion*: there is an opportunity to develop stories with genuine emotional involvement and impact. The Internet can be so much more than pornography and gambling, but it will need writers to get excited about these opportunities and help create meaningful and challenging new forms of drama.

One of the questions for creative web writers is how to envisage these new spaces. Do they just offer a delivery alternative with a difference; a book that can do a few tricks? Is the web a converging media art installation? Or is it a window, like the proscenium arch of a theatre with the audience on an open fourth side altering and goading on the action? Is it solitary game-play entertainment? Is it ontological self-discovery? Do people want choices, or do they want to be told stories?

At the moment, and for the foreseeable future, I suspect there will be more questions than answers.

Part 3

Web writing practicalities

Aladdin has returned home with fruits from the cave which turn out to be precious stones. He rubs the lamp, commanding: 'Fetch me something to eat!' The genie returns with a silver bowl, twelve silver plates containing rich meats, two silver cups, and two bottles of wine. Aladdin's mother, who fainted away at the sight of the genie, says: 'Whence comes this splendid feast?' 'Ask not, but eat,' replied Aladdin.

Parts 1 and 2 of this book drew the wider picture of how different writers are working with the newly evolving media enabled by the web. The reader either needed a lot of imagination to follow the sparks they threw out, or was willing to spend many hours with the book flattened out beside the Internet screen following all the links given in the preceding chapters.

Part 3 gets down to the sentence level and looks at some of the ways in which the very fact that all this is happening on a screen means that we need to write differently. It also gives much-needed information on what software, training or support writers need in order to pursue the ideas in the book to the next stage.

5

Writing style

Creative writing – whether on the web or not – has no rules. It is only in certain genres, such as journalism, twist-ender short stories or Mills & Boon romance, where one can say there are some formulae at work, and not everybody has the ability or desire to be constrained within prescribed writing. Almost every genre welcomes fresh, surprising writing.

Creative writing on the web makes a virtue out of innovation: much of it is designed to shock; to subvert our usual expectations. This means that it plays with language – or 'lexia' as some call it, because words can also be design units in which meaning plays a secondary part to visual appearance. This is all explored more fully in Part 2. So if you are really a Part 2 reader, you can skim through most of this chapter and pick and choose what to pay attention to and what to ignore. That is because it offers conventional, practical detail about what kind of writing works well on the screen. The subversive amongst you may not think that this is an issue, and that it must partly depend on whether there is a narrative or not; but I always feel it's best to reject conventional wisdom on the basis of knowledge. This 'wisdom' comes from a number of sources – university papers, computer companies' research and the accepted guru in this field, Jakob Nielsen, whose Usability Alertbox[57] has information and opinion mostly directed at the commercial world but from which some useful writing principles may be extrapolated (though his own website does not practise what it preaches).

Techniques to increase readability

In the section on readability in Chapter 1 (*see* page 22), I gave some reasons why reading from screens is less efficient than reading from paper. This applies even where you or your publisher have produced

---

[57] <http://www.useit.com/alertbox/>

a nice, clear page layout intended for one of the standard software screen packages (such as Acrobat or Microsoft Reader). Although readers can zoom the text size up or down to suit their own eyesight, there are a number of awkwardnesses about monitors that will slow the reader down. Bear the following in mind:

- The larger the screen, and the better its resolution, the easier it is for the reader to process text.
- If the reader zooms-up the text size, then fewer words appear on the screen. This slows down their reading rate because it is harder to skim-read, which most people do subconsciously while deciding which paragraphs to pay particular attention to.
- Turning over physical pages is superior to scrolling or clicking (and is kinder on the hands, as the mouse movements required for screen reading can result in Repetitive Strain Injury).
- The distance between the reading material and the reader affects reading efficiency, as does the angle of the screen and the position in which the person is sitting. (Although slim laptops may make curling up with an e-book on a computer perfectly possible, the reader still suffers from some of the points listed above.)
- However slight, screen lighting has a flicker, jitter or shimmer that affects the eyes and the ability to read for long periods.

A new e-publisher's idea of typography is typically a PDF file from US letter page size, with Microsoft Word's default of Times Roman 12 point without any leading and set across too wide a measure. This is not ideal for reading from paper, let alone from the screen. Web writer-artists, by contrast, tend to play with typography in ways reminiscent of the magazine typography of the 1970s. They jumble upper and lower case characters, and use experimental spellings and superimpositions, ignoring readability theory altogether. Where there are narrative texts, they tend often to be set in what looks like about 6 point sans-serif (on my high resolution monitor). It is tempting to block-copy and paste into a word-processor, just so that I can read the words – which seems to defeat the idea of web interactivity altogether – and is strictly speaking creating an illegal copy (though it could be argued that this is the similar to time-shift copying which allows users to copy for more convenient consumption at a different time).

Because all of the above work against you as an author, any

creative texts that have a narrative and are expected to function on a screen may have to be written in ways that make it easier for the reader to read. Some of these may compromise your own writing style; others may not.

We have already discussed the difficulties of graphic design on the web in Chapter 1, but there *are* techniques for improving readability and, as many creative web writers are likely to be involved in layout as well as writing, it is worth looking at those first as they are easier to deal with than matters of style.

Colour

Writers should get advice about colour from a designer who understands the principles of web-safe colours. In essence, this is based on RGB, which simply stands for Red, Green and Blue – nature's three primary colours. Monitors and television sets transmit RGB – after all, colour is light – so the only colours available are the ones which standard monitors can transmit. There are 216 'web-safe' colours[58]. Any other colours will behave oddly on some screens (they may go grey, or dither) and there is no guarantee that your monitor will show the same hue of, say, red as mine. Here are some points to bear in mind:

- The contrast ratio between characters and background should be as sharp as possible, and most research suggests that black lettering on a white or pale cream background is the easiest to read. White on black or dark blue also has a high contrast, but the type might look better in bold or in a slightly larger size because colours behave differently in different relationships to each other. Colour combinations that do not work – though ubiquitously used by experimental writers – are white text on red, yellow on black, pink on blue, red on pale grey, green on orange, and so on. It's liberating to be able to knock the conventions of black-and-white print, but it should be on the basis of an understanding of colour theory and of how any two colours react with each other. Take into account the high incidence of colour blindness as well (difficulty in distinguishing between red and green being the most common).
- Background watermarks (very popular in the early days of web design) are now universally regarded as an impediment to

[58] <http://www.visibone.com/colorlab/>

reading. The brain tends to reject anything that is difficult to assimilate.

- The colour of hyperlinks follows the same thinking as above. Some people say that blue underlining is a useful standard because most people now understand that this denotes a link to another section of text. I don't think that this will suit the need for freedom of the creative writer, but aesthetics should still come into any choice. For example, I have seen many creative sites where the hyperlinking text merges so closely into the background colour once the user has clicked that it is then unreadable if you return to the page. This may be useful as an intentional device; otherwise it's just an irritant.

For most creative writing purposes, these points are perhaps all you need to be aware of. For experimental writing, as discussed in Part 2 a much wider knowledge of the colour palette is needed.

Typesetting

Screen fonts were discussed on page 2. Typesetting, as it is known from print, is virtually impossible on the web. Forget about kerning (the hair spaces between letters), about orphans and widows (short lines at the top or the bottom of the page) and the subtleties of leading (distance between lines). But there are some simple things that can be done to improve readability:

- Hyphenation at the end of lines slows down reading and is best avoided. That may mean avoiding right-hand justified text as it is much harder to control on screens of varying sizes.
- Reading is slower with upper case characters, so sentence-case headings (capital intitial letter only) are generally better.
- Fonts with strong ascenders and descenders and a good rounded x-height show up better on screen than thin skimpy fonts.
- Blocks of italics are harder to read than normal text.
- An easy-reading line length is 10–12 words to the line, depending on the size. It is hard to control this on a web page and the only way to do it is to put the text in invisible tables. If you don't know how to do this, consult an HTML guide[59].
- On web pages, you cannot control screen margins except in a percentage ratio to the text area. Some people put an image

[59] Try <http://www.htmlprimer.com/>

the same colour as the background in the left-hand column of a table to act as a spacer. It is worth experimenting to see what works best (while remembering that how it appears on your monitor will be one of many different possibilities).

- Always put a single space after a full-stop on web texts. Extra white space between sentences breaks their natural rhythm. Books and newspapers don't add space, but typing teachers seem to teach people to put two or three spaces after a full point. More space makes the sentences float apart, making life difficult for the reader.

Planning

Whether you are creating a website from which to sell your own print-bound works, or putting together an interactive web-based piece, there are number of planning points worth considering:

- Find and evaluate other websites that display creative work within your own area of interest, and consider what works and what does not. The standard advice to any budding writer is to read a lot and to absorb what others have done in the same genre. It is the same with websites. If you want to write well for the web, look at sites like the one you are going to create. What do you like about them and what does not work for you? The sites given in the listing on pp.143–7 offer some starting points that could occupy you for many hours.
- Decide what you want the web creation to achieve – for yourself and for your audience. If you have this firmly in view, then you have a better chance of creating a successful piece. If the purpose is personal journalism (as in the blogs described on pp. 52–6) then this may be an aim in itself, or you might want to consider it as a possible art-form. If, on the other hand, you are creating a site whose purpose is to sell print-based materials, then the purpose of the site will be a marketing one.
- Draw an overview of the whole thing. Some find this easier on paper and others like an all-through computer solution (mind-mapping software, for example, can take you through ways of thinking about goals and objectives).
- Decide from the beginning how much interaction you want to allow. Do you want to guide the reader down a limited number of branches from the tree? Do you want to create a

randomising effect with multiple links? Do you want to control your visitor with timed displays or single-option clicks?

As you begin to build your website:

- Test the functionality on a friend or colleague to see if the hypertext elements work in the way you had in mind.
- Test the site using as many browsers as you can (try alternative screen resolutions, and Macs or PC in different flavours).
- If you are using artwork or quotations from work that is not your own, think about the copyright implications before you get too far with the project. Retrospective copyright clearance can be tedious and disappointing (if it isn't given or takes too long). It is always easiest to request usage at the same time as you acquire the materials – and keep strict records.
- Advertise by linking to writing communities, other like-minded sites and anywhere appropriate. It is sometimes worth writing a short article for a free e-zine in exchange for a link.

Headings

The art of writing menu-headings for websites is underestimated. It is completely different from the old newspaper technique of grabbing attention with bold, baffling, witty, cryptic or intriguing headings in large type. Menu-headings and hyperlink wording can be easily misunderstood, and the plainer and more obvious they are, the less ambiguous. Ambiguity is particulary irksome on web pages because the user may click on a link with certain expectations and be irritated if they are not fulfilled.

So it is worth taking some care over your choice of any words – headings, buttons and inter-text hyperlinks that lead to documents or other sub-headings on the same or another page. Do they clearly indicate what the user will find by following that choice? Can they be misunderstood? Have you checked that you use the same phrase each time to lead to a page? (If not, your reader will think that there is something new and be frustrated if it leads to a page they have already seen.) In certain creative contexts, it may be your intention to loop back to the same place on different word-clicks. But make sure that this is intentional and not through lack of thinking up:

- synonyms and other ways of expressing the same concept;

- ways in which someone might misunderstand your heading (even a simple word like 'Help' may lead to different expectations);
- simplifications for people for whom English is a second language (after all, this is a global audience and you want your work to reach as wide a readership as possible);
- what the menu-words sound like (remember that the blind may be using synthesised speech technology so make sure the sound is unambiguous too).

One of the more frustrating web activities, I have found, is searching for contact details on a website. Whether or not you are willing to give out your email address is a matter of choice, but a web artwork should always have some equivalent of an imprint on it so that viewers know where it is coming from and how to track down more information. What are we going to call an imprint in this non-print medium? And an informational or functional website should have contact or ownership details available at one click's remove from any page. The choices I have seen include these (and no doubt others):

Contact
Email
Publisher details
Author details
Feedback
Support
Help
Information
End

As web works proliferate, perhaps we can try to come up with standards matching the type of information normally on the back of the title page of a printed book.

Menu choices or headings shown as graphics only are very common on creative sites. Here again, some signs or symbols will mean different things to people from different cultural or ethnic backgrounds; so if it is important to convey a meaning that does not confuse the viewer, then some 'hover text' that pops up when the mouse hovers over a graphic may be a way of clarifying this. There are different ways of creating hover text (most commonly text alternatives using the ALT code; title code; JavaScript).

Hyperlinking

Links are really only electrified contents pages, footnotes, cross-references or indexes. With the exception of some (few) original creative writing experiments, there is almost nothing the Internet adds to informational text that does not occur in the book or magazine world. It's simply a more convenient way of jumping about. That's all hyperlinking is on most websites.

If you have an essentially informational purpose, don't put too many links within the text. You want your reader to stay with you to absorb your point, not dash off somewhere else just because there's a link. So try to keep lists of links in one place – elsewhere on the page as 'see also' material or even on a separate links page. When it is useful to embed a link to extra information in the text, keep the link-words as short as possible (2–4 words only) so that the eye can instantly absorb them.

It is safe to assume that the reader will understand that underlining, or a different colour text, indicates a hyperlink. So I think it is better style to avoid redundant phrases like these:

Click here to enter
Click on this
Select this
Click here

However, 'Skip intro', 'Skip pre-load' and other 'how to avoid time-consuming sound and graphics loading' link-words are useful. The convention is to use blue for the link and purple for a visited link – that's a design decision and audiences are sophisticated enough now to adapt to any colour.

The title code gives a brief description of what readers can expect if they click on the link, and appears as hover text when the user rests the cursor on the link. The title code is not necessarily the same as the page title. Let's imagine it is for the page you are reading now. One could put:

<title>Dorner: Creative Web Writing – Chapter 5: Hyperlinking</title>

or just

<title>Hyperlinking</title>

The second is clearly too general. When someone comes to a website that they would like to bookmark, the words within the <title>

</title> code will appear in the Bookmark or Favourites listing. So you are giving more information to your user if you have a longer, explanatory title. They'll remember what the page was and why they saved the link. Use this sparingly as it puts the onus on the reader to hover over the link and is yet another thing to do. It also slows the loading of the page (but only fractionally). Ten words of title code are more than enough. Information to use in a link title includes:

- the name of the site if it is not the current one;
- the title of the creative work;
- warnings if a page is password-protected;
- descriptive detail you don't want to put in the text subdirectory if the site has a complex tree structure.

Paragraphing

Breaking up text into paragraph-units is a visual device much needed for screen-reading. Fowler's *Modern English Usage* says of the paragraph:

> The purpose of paragraphing is to give the reader a rest. The writer is saying to him: 'Have you got that? If so, I'll go on to the next point.' Paragraphing is also a matter of the eye. A reader will address himself more readily to his task if he sees from the start that he will have breathing space from time to time than if what is before him looks like a marathon course.

In book and magazine typesetting, the normal style is to start with text full out after a heading and then indent every subsequent paragraph. That doesn't work well on web pages (though you may revert to it for PDF files designed with paper reading in mind). On the web, it is best to use the word-processing technique of double carriage returns. White space helps web display so if you write in 'chunks' of 30-word paragraphs it tends to help the eye. But vary paragraph lengths so that the eye can easily take in the point and can orientate on a scrolling page.

In informational texts, readers want to grasp the main point at the top of the screen: it saves time. They'll move on if nothing grabs their attention. Remember that they may only see the first paragraph without scrolling down so it is particularly vital to get to the point quickly. Techniques you can use to be concise include:

- lists;
- short phrases, not full sentences;
- brief statements.

A list like this is easy to take in at a glance, but balance that against the number of lines it is going to take up on the screen. Every line near the top of a web page must earn its shelf space. Make sure that you are not providing too little information in the effort to be concise.

In creative texts, a paragraph usually forms the basis of a single screen chunk (or lexia, defined more fully on pp. 72–3). The creator generally designs the work so that these chunks pop up in separate (or maybe overlapping) screens and so controls how much text will be on the screen at any one time.

Summaries

A writer's skill in writing quick-flash summaries is paramount. You have just a handful of words to let readers know the scope and type of information (or book blurb) that is lower down the page, or on another one.

On an informational page, you ideally want to provide enough information so that the visitor doesn't have to read any more. This is the essence of functional web style. It is more flexible and more practical than print style, though the aim is still the same: to make the reader's task easy, even if this means extra work for you. In fact, print is really the wrong model. Think of other media; the overall word-count of a 20-minute radio or television documentary is about a third of 20 minutes of reading from print. A web summary should be even shorter.

Brevity

Every creative writer has personal views on style. Some of the 'Nouveaux Bloomsbury' innovators whose work I have quoted in this book have developed web-specific styles based on inventive use of non-grammar-based keyboard characters or insertion of coding within the text. If you are concerned with informational writing, however, there are a few simple thoughts to bear in mind.

Web writing style depends on context, but everyone's aim is to save keystrokes. 'Cut to the quick,' is the motto. The expense and eye-strain of online reading demands it. So consider these points:

- **Know your audience**: know who you are writing for before you begin, and plan accordingly.
- **Start with your main points**: hit your reader with the salient points at the top of the web page (people are reluctant to scroll). Use interior pages to unfold details and complexity.
- **Be concise**: cut every word that doesn't contribute. A good web-page length is under 200 words – it is better to divide anything longer than that into sub-topics. You can also have a 'print friendly' version so that an article that would run to 10 pages or so in 200-word chunks can be printed in one go without stepping through several screens.
- **Write simple sentences**: ideas are easier to digest in a simple subject-verb-object progression. Make sub-clauses into separate sentences. Use one idea per sentence and keep sentences under 17 words (the average for print).
- **Use specific words**: 'red and blue' is better than 'multi-coloured'; 'snow and sleet' is better than 'bad weather'.
- **Use plain words**: 'began', 'said', 'end' rather than 'commenced', 'expressed' or 'terminated'.
- **Be direct**: The web is friendly. Use 'we' and 'you' instead of 'the insured', 'the applicant', 'the society' and so on. It is also more direct to use the present tense rather than the passive.
- **Be positive**: 'the web works well' rather than 'the web doesn't function badly'.

Humour

Generally speaking, humour, irony and literary devices do not work well on the screen, possibly because it is more widely used for functional reading than for literary reading. The result is that the dreadful multiple exclamation mark (as noted below) is ubiquitous. This is either because insecure writers do not know what its proper use is or because humour on the screen needs flagging. A sentence that falls flat without an exclamation mark is a flat sentence. If it's funny, the reader will notice. Adding one, two or three 'screamers' (as newspaper men used to call them) will not tell the reader that the sentence was funny; it will only limpingly point out that it was meant to be funny.

Yet writers want to be informal on the web, because it is a democratic and widely inclusive medium – so there's a vogue for simplified spelling, much over-use of the letter 'zed', a tendency to write in all the 'err's and 'um's and 'yeah, well, like…' phrases that scribblers have hitherto excised from written forms. Harsh though this may sound, facetiousness is hardly ever witty; it's generally just padding and the mark of unconsidered writing.

Punctuation

The new technologies of word-processors and web-display are subtly altering printed language. We seem to be returning to the Elizabethan style, when compositors often varied the spelling of words in order to justify a line of type, so that it fitted the right length. Their readers were used to seeing the same word spelled in different ways on the same page. The same tendencies occur on the web.

Dashes show up better on the screen and obviate the necessity for distinguishing between colons and semi-colons. Sophisticated punctuation will probably cease to be used. Display headings add apostrophes in non-possessive plurals. Some of the web-common punctuation marks are printed overleaf.

Foreign-accent setting is achieved with difficulty on screens. The chances are that words which are generally accepted and understood in English usage – such as cliché – will eventually lose their accents.

Other keyboard marks are coming into use in email and e-zines – not to separate sentences into understandable parts, but as attention-seekers to make headings stand out or to separate paragraphs, e.g.:

>>> My cat <<<
{} ****** {}{}{}{} ****** {}
| |=| |=| |=| |=| |=| |=| |=| |

Such matters present a challenge for authors and publishers to reassess the ways in which language is developing and what repercussions the need to read on screens will have on language. This is why so many net experimentalists are using keyboard characters in a variety of new ways in order to redefine language assumptions. After all, this has happened throughout the history of language, and will continue to happen.

Sign	Name	Usage
~	tilde	used in web addresses and as separators between words or lines
#	hash	used in hyperlinks within a web page
/	slash	used as separators
\	backslash	used as separators
|	pipe	has no function in everyday text (on web pages, it separates items on the same line in a link-list at the top or left-hand side of the screen)
—	underscore	used for book titles to indicate italics
*	asterisk	signals highly stylised, even artistic varieties of textual substitution for traditionally non-verbal information. (In chatrooms, for instance, asterisks often enclose stage directions where people are attempting to give each other the visual and vocal clues commonplace in everyday discourse. For example, you might write *hollow laughter* to indicate that a statement is ironic, *yawn* to indicate sleepiness, or *pleading look* when you are asking someone for a favour. Clearly the conventions will settle over time resulting in a redefinition of the way in which people write)
.	dot	part of a web address, and also entering the language as a noun and in verbal forms.
>>		next page
<<		previous page
--	double hyphen	used instead of the two typesetting dashes: en-dash – (coded as –) or em-dash — (coded as —). Typographers use thin spaces before and after an en-dash (not achievable in HTML) and no spaces on each side of an em-dash
[ ]	brackets	these are changing shape: it is easier for non-typists to use square brackets because they are on the lower shift of a computer keyboard
•	bullet points	look good on screens and are useful aids to clarity because the eye grows weary reading across the screen. In print, too many lists get tedious; on screen they act as a cosmetic aid. Nested lists can convey information quickly
!!!	exclamation	in triplicate these are becoming common – there's even a punctuation mark called the 'interrobang', created in 1962 to fill a gap in our punctuation system for rhetorical statements where neither the question nor an exclamation alone exactly served the writer (as in 'How about that?!'). Will it catch on? You will find it on Microsoft fonts Wingdings 2

Editing

It is always best to do a final edit on paper, but many people are quite happy editing first on screen. It depends what kind of writer you are. As the Introduction describes, some compose by getting down their ideas as quickly as possible without worrying too much about accuracy, coherence and finesses of expression, which are all tidied up in subsequent edits. Others craft as they write, polishing while composing. Sometimes there is a pendulum-swing effect as the 'editorial persona' sweeps backwards and forwards across what the 'ideas persona' has said, reviewing backwards while adding forwards.

Whatever one's personal method, there will always be a final edit when the piece is ready. For all the reasons above about the superiority of reading on paper compared with reading on screens, I would always, always edit on paper. It just reads differently.

It is easier to edit someone else's text than it is your own. Somehow one can see, with blinding clarity, how a few small structural changes will make the flow of an argument clear: but look at your own, and you can't see the wood for the trees. You get fond of words or phrases that you want to keep and get offended when others don't appreciate them. You don't even see your own spelling mistakes. These are called 'literals' in the trade, which is a kind way of saying that of course it's the keyboard that can't spell, not you.

The writer needs to bow down to the household god of editing: consistency. Copy-editing isn't prized on the web, so the writer must fulfil that nit-picky role. It's all to do with getting the message across and making sure that the reader understands. The site visitor irritated by a typo, ambiguity, PR-speak or inconsistency is not a well-disposed reader. Of course, it's hard to monitor on the web, as it's a dynamic medium and it's easy to forget consistency choices made on a previous update.

In an ideal world, everyone needs an editor – someone who comes fresh to the writing and sees the strengths and faults with clarity. Even if you have a third eye, you should still learn to read your own work critically and do as much editing as you can yourself.

House style

Edit to a house style. Even those who work alone will find it useful to draw up word-lists and house-style rules so that you have a reference point for consistency throughout a long piece. Word-lists include words that have alternative spellings, such as: acknowledgement/acknowledgment; appendixes/appendices; centring/centering; disk/disc; enquiry/inquiry; focused/focussed; judgement/judgment; indexes/indices; -ise or -ize spellings; and so on/etc.

Other matters of house style that apply particularly to screen works are given below – and if you are engaged on a collaborative web work of any kind, drawing up a list like this should be something you do very early on. The 'e.g.' suggestions provided do not, of course, apply to experimental works, but experimentalists should nevertheless be aware of what the usability research, on which they are based, advises.

Text
e.g. Verdana, Arial, Sans Serif or Normal – preferably use a Cascading Style Sheet.

Sheet template
Size: e.g. 10 pt, small, size 1.
Colour: e.g. black.
Background colour: e.g. white.

Line length
Constrained by the pixel width of the table, but ideally about 10–12 words per line, depending on the length of word.

Borders
e.g. no borders (BORDER=0).

Paragraphs
Spacing: e.g. spacing between paragraphs to be 1 blank line.
Headings: e.g. avoid headings entirely in upper case. First letter capitalised. Consistent naming throughout site.

Page length
No more than two 640 x 480 screens-worth of information where possible. Length of text to be compatible with printing on not more than one sheet of A4.

The *Yale Style Manual*[60] recommends that the 'safe' area on a screen for display purposes only should be no more than 600 pixels

---

[60] <http://www.med.yale.edu/caim/manual/> (worth looking at – a second edition with updated web advice was imminent as I wrote this book)

wide. They recommend 535 pixels as the maximum width for page layouts which are to be printed (though my own view is that you can go up to 700). This is the widest table that will print on standard A4 paper without cropping the text in the right-hand column.

Italics
Use for book titles, film titles, emphasis. Avoid for body text. In emails decide between *title* and _title_ for quoting references.

Quote marks
UK style favours single quotation marks ' ' , to be used sparingly and set properly (Word calls them 'smart' quotes). They are difficult to code on websites, but the cognoscenti may be offended by the straight prime mark (unsmart or straight quotation mark). Try these HTML codes (unfortunately they may not show up correctly on every browser):

Left single quote	&#145;
Right single quote or apostrophe	&#146;
Left double quote	&#147;
Right double quote	&#148;

Links
Decide whether to:

- underline them (a useful convention because people understand it, and also because underlined links show up when people print out the page. Creative web artists, however, often like to make their readers guess what the link-words are, so their aim can be to get as far from convention as possible);
- include the http:// protocol in listings (the trouble with leaving them out is that not all URLs start with www and it can be difficult to decide how to set those);
- show the full URL on the screen or hide it behind the URL page title. I used to hide them, but I now prefer to make the URL visible because visitors can gain information from the different parts of the address that helps them to decide the level of trust to place in that source;
- include the angle brackets in references < > (as I do in this book because it is now becoming a standard to do so in scholarly texts, and having standards is helpful).

Exclamation marks

Use exclamation marks only for a genuine exclamation, e.g. 'Poppycock!' not 'And that's a fact!' – but 'Yahoo!', because that is how the company spells its name.

Capitalisation

Capitals look worse on screens than on paper. Choose between these (the first being my preference for screens):

> Decide on heading styles

or

> Decide on Heading Styles

but not

> Decide On Heading Styles

or

> DECIDE ON HEADING STYLES

Intercaps such as 'aVANT-pOP' are for experimental sites. Optional: ftp or FTP; PDF or pdf; MUDs & MOOs or Muds and Moos – even though these derive from abbreviations.

Hyphenation

Follow a good spelling dictionary, but be prepared to close up words as they go into common usage, e.g. email not e-mail. The web mantra is 'save keystrokes'. Use hyphens for clarity, as in:

- compound adjectives: top-level domain name;
- onscreen command: drag-and-drop;
- commands: Control-Alt-Delete.

Units of measurement

Follow normal conventions. Typically, there is no space between the unit and the number: 600MHz, 1400dpi, 128k. MB and Mb have become optional although Mb is technically correct.

Finally, some further writing tips from a circulated anonymous joke email makes several other points quite amusingly:

> Avoid alliteration. Always.
> Never use a long word when a diminutive one will do.
> Parenthetical remarks (however relevant) are unnecessary.
> Remember to never split an infinitive.

Contractions aren't necessary.

Foreign words and phrases are not apropos.

One should never generalise.

Don't be redundant; don't use more words than necessary; it's highly super-fluous.

Be more or less specific.

One-word sentences? Eliminate.

The passive voice is to be avoided.

Even if a mixed metaphor sings, it should be derailed.

Who needs rhetorical questions?

Exaggeration is a billion times worse than understatement.

Proof-read carefully to see if you words out.

A writer must not shift your point of view.

And don't start a sentence with a conjunction. (Remember, too, that a preposition is a terrible word to end a sentence with.)

Don't overuse exclamation marks!!!!!!!

Writing carefully, dangling participles must be avoided.

Last but not least, avoid clichés like the plague; they're old hat; seek viable alternatives.

Electronic editing

There is no such thing as automatic editing, of course, but you can use word-processor routines for the following:

- search and replace to achieve consistency – e.g. e-mail or email, on-line or online (both are acceptable, though one strong view is that when a word goes into general usage there is no longer any need to hyphenate, so I personally prefer 'email' but 'e-book');
- word-count to monitor your preferred page length;
- grammar and spelling checker as a first 'throw' at weeding out errors (you will have to read intelligently as well) – I prefer to run this after the first draft as I find it distracting to have the checkers running as I type;
- turn on Track Changes (also known as the Reviewing toolbar) if you want to show others what alterations you have made, or if you need to review changes made by another reader on the document you are working on. In Microsoft Word this is in the Tools menu (but do be careful with the Merge Document function on post-2000 versions of Word, because it has a mind

of its own) – other programs may call this function Edit Trace, Document Comparison or Redlining;

- Autocorrect standard errors on the fly, such as common mistypings, like 'teh' or 'abuot', or 'adn'. Add your own, or use this function as a short-cut to longer phrases;
- replace double hyphens with an en-dash or em-dash, and replace straight quotes with 'smart' quotes. This is better done in the word-processor if you are planning to block-copy the text into a graphical web-creation package, as many of them handle dashes and quotation marks very poorly (*see* also Punctuation, above).

Make sure you get a right single quote in omissions, e.g. in the '90s. Your word-processor will get this wrong so block-copy the correct mark from the end of the numeral and paste it in front. We all know that 90's is wrong but it is so often seen like that on websites (and even on the Queen's Jubilee history procession floats) that it may eventually become accepted usage.

Accessibility

New-media writing eschews convention, and ultimately this could lead to exciting results. But it's undemocratic to be nonchalant about accessibility issues. Large numbers of creators don't care whether texts are legible on screens of resolutions other than the ones they set them up in, or whether the colours allow maximum readability – I have seen so many with minute writing in, say, shocking pink on a Thatcher-blue background or vivid yellow trailing into red. The creators don't care if the user doesn't have the latest version of Flash or Shockwave, or RealAudio, or if it takes minutes to load the splash page (decorative first page) – and they certainly are not interested in equal opportunity for anyone physically disadvantaged. In fact, even experimental writing can supply some 'wheelchairs and ramps'. As the W3 Web content Accessibility Guidelines[61] put it:

> The architect designed the building with both elevators and stairs. Some people prefer to take stairs, while some people find the stairs too challenging or impossible. On your website, some people will prefer images, animations, multimedia, fast-paced interactive games, while others will find

[61] <http://www.w3.org/tr/wai-webcontent>

them too challenging or impossible to use. As with elevators and stairs, provide a variety of ways for people to access and to navigate through your web content.

To do that, you might want to review your work to see if you have provided:

- one or more navigation mechanisms for people who can't see very well, or can't hear properly, or can't use a mouse;
- text equivalents for all non-text content (e.g. use the ALT [alternative text] tag for images, collated text transcripts for audio and video-streaming, descriptions for animations, a static form as well as interactive scripts);
- some other labels identifying the content;
- speech-synthesis capacity for people who can't read labels easily;
- the capacity for words to be highlighted as they are read.

Think about accessibility – some people still have slow Internet access and choose not to download images. And partially sighted users, who can use their browser settings to increase the font size, might not get the version of the text arrangement that you want. They may also not be able to read the graphic versions of the menus, since these are unaffected by browser text settings.

Online chat etiquette

There is a level of flippancy and informality in web writing and email that has become acceptable discourse; it's OK to be informal. All the same, people are still people and the same rules of social awareness apply. If you wouldn't say something face-to-face, don't do it in an online community chatroom. It's very easy to feel detached from what you are keying onto a screen, partly because there is the multiple distancing of silence, inherent problems of decoding text, lack of communication cues, and uncertainty about what time-lags mean. If you are in an interactive writing environment, you might want to bear in mind the following points:

- Read contributions twice before sending, in case there's anything unclear or offensive in them.
- Avoid expressing strong feelings of disagreement in public forums.

- Ask permission before forwarding or copying other people's contributions – they're not yours (this applies to email too).
- Avoid sexist or racist language.
- When contributing to a collaborative interactive work that has been in existence for some time, read through all the contributions to date to avoid asking a question or making a point that has already been made.
- Do not assume that all outrageous contributions are intended to inflame opinion (they may be a clumsy attempt at humour or a lack of familiarity with the medium).
- Avoid writing all in upper case (it looks as if you are SHOUTING). Using all lower case is quite common online to save time.
- Use short paragraphs; people are overwhelmed by large pieces of text. Short, coherent chunks allow readers to 'breathe' and also give relief to the eye.

Acknowledging sources

The same rules of citation apply to research material found on the Internet as anywhere else. The format you use depends on the discipline of your own subject area and will match the bibliographical styles (e.g. the academic conventions of the Harvard, Chicago, MLA and APA styles, and many more). All are different in detail, but the following principles apply to quoting web-originated materials.

- Make sure that a reader can find the source you are citing.
- The citation for a web document often follows a format similar to that for print, with some information omitted and some added. E.g.:

Author/editor. (Year). Title [online]. (Edition). Place of publication, Publisher (if ascertainable). Available from:
URL [Accessed Date].
e.g. Dorner, J. (2001). Citation formats [online]. Available from:
<http://www.internetwriter.co.uk/chapters/chap5_edit.htm#cite>
[Accessed 8 Mar 2002].

If you cannot find some elements of information, cite what is available. E.g.:
Instead of a title, there may only be a file name.

The place of publication and the name of the publisher may be replaced online by the URL.

If the work was originally for print, it may be necessary to give the date of the original print publication.

Online authors may only use login names or aliases.

- Always include the date on which you accessed the source (equivalent to the edition) as indicated above.
- Cite the complete address (URL) accurately (within angled brackets is the MLA style). Include the access-mode (http, ftp, telnet, etc.). If you have to divide the URL between two lines, break only after a slash mark and do not insert a hyphen at the break.
- URLs do, unfortunately, change. Researchers generally realise that they may have to step back to the core domain name in a URL that has several directory layers.
- Referencing emails is in this recommended form:
  Sender (Sender's email address). (Day Month Year). Subject of Message. Email to Recipient (Recipient's email address).

  e.g. Dorner, J. (jane@editor.net). (5 Mar 2002).
  Quoting email References. Email to A. Taylor .... (a.taylor@acblack.com).

- On your own website, it is a good idea to have an acknowl-edgement statement with some wording like this:

  The contents of these pages are <sitename> and contributors 2003, 2004. This site was structured, edited and designed by <names in the team>

Legal detail

Much new-media writing has developed without paying sufficient attention to legal detail, though this is rapidly changing. Stuart Moulthrop, for example, obtained literary acclaim for his 'Forking Paths' hypertext in 1987 but has now withdrawn it from view because it contains much of the text of Jorge Luis Borges's short story, 'The Garden of Forking Paths' from *Ficciones* (1941). His website says:

  I don't believe it should be published or otherwise circulated without per-mission of the copyright holders. Since the hypertext was a limited experiment that long since served its purpose, I have not sought permis-sion. I no longer use or circulate this text.

The laws of copyright apply to the Internet exactly as they do to print and I have written much about this elsewhere (*The Internet: A Writer's Guide*, A & C Black, 2001). There has traditionally been an honour system among writers and some have always abused it with or without technologies. Plagiarism was rife and now is rifer. But the technology has made it too easy to cover one's tracks. You can even twist and twiddle 'borrowed' paragraphs automatically, and without much thought, by using grammar-checkers, thesauri, translation programs and so on. It's equally easy for even the most careful and morally conscious writer to be unaware that a section of text rediscovered in a personal file is not their original work. It isn't simply that the technology is fudging boundaries, but that technology itself is responsible for a cultural shift in what it is to be a writer; what it is to confront original text.

It would be retrogressive if we simply travelled backwards in time and returned to a climate of free-for-all – though some web experimentalists would have it so, using the argument that if you cannot protect intellectual property on the web, you might as well make appropriation a virtue. Too many interests seem to controvert that theory. It may have been an acceptable convention for Bach to grab and embellish on some lesser composer's theme; nor did anyone sue Handel when he scooped up any number of previously existing works (by himself or others) and cut-and-pasted them into his latest opera. And perhaps Metastasio was content that *Artaxerses* was set to music 45 times with no Performing Rights Society weighing in for his cut. But times have radically changed. Try quoting a handful of identifiable words, or ten consecutive notes, from a modern pop-song and your permissions bill would be prohibitive. The music industry is throwing more money at protection mechanisms than writer support groups can afford. It is taking a very long time, but I have confidence that one day, secure systems will be in place.

There are one or two points worth drawing to the attention of writers who have personal websites, traditional or experimental. For a comprehensive source of information, see IP – the government-backed home of UK Intellectual Property on the Internet.[62]

---

[62] <http://www.intellectual-property.gov.uk>

Web-specific issues

1. Quite a lot of material has been put on the web without the permission of the copyright owners. You should therefore be cautious about using any material on the web, although if the site is hosted by someone you trust then it is probably reasonable to assume that the material has been put on the site with permission. Project Gutenberg and the Oxford Text Archive, for example, carry information on the copyright status of their electronic texts.

2. If in doubt whether you can use material on the web in a work of your own, email the owner of the site and ask. Generally, permission will be granted for educational or experimental uses.

3. A short extract of a work or a web page can be used with acknowledgement for the purposes of criticism and review without seeking permission. There is no real agreeement about what 'short' means, so if in doubt it's always safest to ask.

4. Parody, homage, satire, burlesque and caricature are not regarded as plagiarism, but be very careful, as there is a fine line. The law exists to protect originators, but it is not intended that it should stop the free flow of humorous and artistic reference – viz. T S Eliot's half-quotes and pastiches in *The Waste Land*.

5. Although it has long been within the spirit of web writing to catalogue links (web-logs being a prime example of this), hyperlinking has some grey areas of uncertainty. It is almost always acceptable to link to a site's front page, but links to inside pages – or links to a page or image on the linked site that appears to the reader to be part of your page – are best not done without permission, because users may not immediately realise what is your material and what is not, or even when they are leaving your site. It's best to open up another browser window for linked sites or to include a notice telling viewers that they are leaving your site.[63]

6. If you know or suspect that a site linked to yours includes material that is illegal in any way, such as it is defamatory or infringes copyright, you should break the link immediately, otherwise you could be liable too. You always need to think carefully about what you link to.[64]

7. Under English law, if you link to third-party material which is defamatory you may be liable for publishing it. It is unlikely that a disclaimer would make any difference to that.

[63] <http://www.cla.co.uk/copyrightvillage/internet.html>

[64] <http://www.twobirds.com/library/internet/disc.htm>

8. Generally speaking, a simple link to another website is not considered as infringement. However, when a link also contains a title and some text, infringement may take place and clearance is probably required.

9. Make sure that you keep adequate records of where material has come from and how you have used it, in case you are ever challenged by copyright owners and have to show that you have tried to be compliant.

10. Software code is also copyrighted as literary works, so tempting as it is to 'borrow' JavaScript or other interactive coding from other sites, resist – or write and ask if you may. Surprisingly, some web authors are very generous – as long as they are duly acknowledged. There are plenty of free resources where owners have made their code freely available.[65]

11. Email and items in chatrooms or web boards are 'literary works' as well and belong to the writer. This means that others should not forward them to anyone else without permission.

12. Establish the rules of ownership in any collaborative writing projects before you start to write.

13. Although your own work is in copyright as soon as you write it and does not need to be registered with any particular agency, it is still good practice to tell visitors to your site what your own conditions are. The form of words I use is:

> You may print or download extracts from these pages to a local hard disk for your personal use only, provided that none of the text is altered or manipulated. If you recopy the material to individual third parties, we would like you to:
>
> • acknowledge <sitename> as the source of the material;
> and
> • inform any third parties that these conditions apply to them also.

14. When authoring a website either of your own work or in collaboration with others, consider whether you need any of the following and consult a lawyer if you think you do:

- Credits and permissions
- Copyright statement
- Disclaimers
- Privacy statements

---

[65] <http://www.cgi-resources.com>

- Terms and conditions of use
- E-commerce encryption assurances
- Statement of statutory rights

There was a time when writers addressed the public inclusively as 'Dear Reader' or 'Gentle Reader'. Everyone felt valued as the author's friend – they were engaged, jointly, in an act of complicity. They agreed to stay with the writer, if not from first page to last then at least following the argument from unfolding to conclusion. Readers appreciated clarity of argument as well as the wiles of stylistic device designed to keep them excited.

But the Internet is not the place for sequential reading. According to research in rhetoric linguistics, 'reader expectation theory' demands writing that economises on 'reader energy'. All this means is that good structure and word choice are paramount; they always were, but 'cut to the quick' is the motto of web writing. So, to summarise this chapter, expectations now are that the writer will:

- put the whole argument at the top of the screen;
- bullet-point, number, or list ideas for quick visibility (like this);
- break details into discrete chunks;
- offer rapid click-links to more information somewhere else.

On screens, visitors no longer *read* a text – as in 'study, familiarise', but rather scan it looking only for what is useful to them. Rapid-reading tutors used to teach politicians and businessmen to skim-read diagonally across the page. Now, they scan websites.

The sections in this chapter show a need to be brief, but not bland or rude. Writing with flair in a medium that demands brevity presents a challenge. As ever, the maxim is, 'hard writing, easy reading'. We would all do well to remember that readers are essentially visitors; they may drop in and look around, but if nothing grabs their attention sufficiently, they will drift off somewhere else. This remains true whether you offer fiction, drama, poetry, non-fiction or an informational website.

6

Listings

Note: Most of the technical terms used in these pages are explained in my book *The Internet: A Writer's Guide* (A & C Black, 2nd Edn 2001, £10.99).[66]

Basic equipment needed

A Pentium III or Mac G4 with 128Mb RAM
Broadband or a DSL line (unmetered Internet connections)

Plug-ins:
Flash and Shockwave – play animations, music and interactive puzzles and games
QuickTime – plays audio and video clips
RealAudio – enables sound and music broadcasting
Acrobat Reader – lets you read downloaded publications
Beatnik – lets you play music

Software for self-publishing

Acrobat Distiller creates PDF files from word-processed or desk-top-published pages
Adobe Photoshop is the industry standard imaging and production tool for those interested in multimedia, the web, print and 3D
After Effects is the industry standard for creating 2D motion graphics on desktop computers
Dreamweaver is the state-of-the-art package for web-page creation
JavaScript is a scripting language that makes web pages dynamic
Final Cut Pro (Mac) is a professional film and video editing tool
Flash brings movement, sound and interactivity to web pages

---

[66] <http://www.internetwriter.co.uk/>

Macromedia Director is a sophisticated program for creating animations and moving pictures
3D Studio MAX is a 3D modelling and animation package

Experimental writing software

At the time of writing, there is a lot of free software available from the sites below. Most of it takes 20–30 minutes to download on a fast modem and then needs to be installed. Being free, it is also uncommercial – that is, it takes some perseverance to get the best out of it. I have played with all the free software mentioned here, but I could not say I have got the most out of the products. The fact that none of them has sufficiently excited me, does not mean they won't appeal to someone else, however. Descriptions of the software are lightly edited from the texts on the individual sites, and my added comments are for rough guidance only.

For the sake of completeness, I have also included the major far-from-free authoring packages. These offer trial downloads, but are so hard to get to know that the serious web writer would do better to invest in serious time and money to get good results.

Alice

<http://www.alice.cs.cmu.edu/> 18 Mb download file
Alice is a 3D Interactive Graphics Programming Environment for Windows 95/98/NT built at Carnegie Mellon University. It aims to make it easy for novices to explore the new medium of interactive 3D graphics and interactive story-telling. You can create a virtual world in Alice and interact with it using a web browser. It is said to be for 3D what the Kodak Brownie camera was to photography, in that it allows almost anyone to tell an animated, 3D story 'as easily as creating a web page'. That may be so, but it's not quite as intuitive as one might wish (although perhaps the Brownie box camera wasn't either). You write simple scripts, to control how an object looks and behaves, using mouse and keyboard to move it around. For example, objects will have a front, side, and top (rather than the X, Y, and Z axes that 3D graphics programming forces users to learn) so that you can tell the object to go backwards or turn left (rather than translate in the minus-X direction or rotate around the Z-axis).

This could be a useful tool for students experimenting with using computer graphics as part of a story-telling project.

Blogger

<http://www.blogger.com/>
Blogger is a free, web-based tool for instantly publishing 'blogs' to the web (see also pp. 52–6). The Blogger site makes it very easy to publish to the web without writing any code or worrying about installing any sort of server software or scripts. You simply provide Blogger with a template of your page (or use one of several pre-designed ones) that indicates where you want your postings to appear. When you want to publish something, you simply enter it in a form. When you're ready, you hit a Publish button that will automatically send your new page to your web server. Similar software is at <http://pitas.com/> and <http://groksoup.com/>

Brutus Story Generator

<http://www.rpi.edu/dept/ppcs/BRUTUS/brutus.html>
v. 2 relaunching
Brutus.1 was a fiction-writing program developed by the Minds and Machines Laboratory which reduced concepts, such as betrayal, into a series of algorithms and data structures to create a story generator. Brutus.1 is used in support of the view that computers will never be genuinely creative, but they can be cleverly programmed to 'appear' to be. The creators believe that Artificial Intelligence is moving us towards a real-life version of the movie *Blade Runner*, in which, behaviourally speaking, humans and androids are indistinguishable.

At the time of writing, Brutus.2 is due to relaunch – so I could not try out the generator. However, you can see some results at Instantnovelist.com<http://www.instantnovelist.com/human.html> which has posted five stories, four written by humans and the fifth by Brutus.1. Visitors voted for their favourite story – and on which one they thought was written by a machine. They chose Brutus as the least favourite writer, but only 25% spotted its robotic prose style (though the truth is that none of the stories displays enviable style).

Creativity Unleashed

<http://www.cul.co.uk/>
Software randomisers and games to stimulate creative thinking (free, but there's a book on the theory behind them that the pro-

ducers hope you will buy). Originally intended for business, some of this software could be useful for blocked writers. For example, it uses mind-mapping techniques to generate ideas. In one version of the software, you can opt to look at the idea through someone else's eyes and get a totally different viewpoint.

Director

<http://www.macromedia.com/software/director/>
25 Mb download
Macromedia Director Shockwave Studio is the 'bees knees' of multimedia for creating 3D entertainment, interactive demonstrations and publishing, online learning courses and animated stories of all kinds. There's a 30-day free trial download version, but it is not for the faint-hearted.

Fabula

<http://www.fabula.eu.org/> 8 Mb download file
Fabula is a free software package for making bi-lingual multi-media stories for primary school children. It bolts onto Word and displays in Netscape (not Explorer), and enables teachers, parents and children to combine texts, images and sounds in two languages – the aim being to make fun-to-use interactive learning resources. Text is added to the story through an Edit Page form. The writer inserts text into the ten text fields provided (five for each language). The number of characters you can enter is limited so that the text will fit properly into the text box in the finished version of the story. Image and sound options are added later. An interesting concept which could be taken further than the developmental stage it reached under the EU funding it received in the millennium year.

JavaScript

<http://jsworld.com/>
JavaScript applets are bits of programming that add interactivity to your site – such as things happening on the screen when you roll the mouse over a word; controlling where and how words appear on the screen; bringing up new text when the user clicks a button; randomising what text appears according to the time the user entered the site; and using passwords and many useful entertainment tricks. There are many sources of free applets and the URL

given above is as good a starting point as any. You may wish to exercise good taste in incorporating any of these into your own pages, and best results will necessarily come from writing your own applets (or working with someone who can realise an idea for you).

KidPad

<http://www.kidpad.org/> 12 Mb download file
KidPad is a collaborative story-writing tool for children, in development at the University of Maryland. It provides basic drawing functionality on a zooming canvas (using the engineering software Jazz). The narrative structure of a story is defined by creating spatial hyperlinks between objects on the canvas. Instead of using a standard WIMP (Windows, Icons, Menus, Pointer) user interface, KidPad uses local tools that can be picked up, used and dropped anywhere on the drawing surface. Those with USB ports can connect up several users on their own mouse, each one controlling a tool in KidPad so that several children can work on a story at the same time.

Puppettime

<http://www.puppettime.com> 12 Mb download file
This is a system for story-boarding in 3D and requires Quicktime to run. It offers basic television-style story-telling and film-making techniques. You choose characters, type in a text script and record your own voice; the system generates a sound dialogue with a timeline and you move the characters and cameras around pre-defined sets, choosing some basic animation as you go. The system is fairly primitive at present, but indicates one direction in which things could develop. An important question is how far authors want to fix the appearance of characters and surroundings rather than letting readers create them in their imaginations.

Storycraft

<http://www.writerspage.com/>
Inexpensive, but not free, fiction and screenwriting program that claims to help you turn ideas into complete novels, screenplays, plays or short stories. If the site offered some sample information, one could form a judgement on what the software is like. It is in version 4.

Storyspace

<http://www.eastgate.com/storyspace/> 3 Mb download file
This is an updated version of the first hypertext creation software
(Michael Joyce, who wrote *Afternoon*, was one of the collaborators).
This is a limited-function demo version lasting a useful three months,
after which you must buy it. Storyspace is a hypertext writing environment, designed for the process of writing rather than visual
presentation. It works on a quasi file-card system, offering spaces for
text lexia. Writing spaces can contain text, pictures and other media
and link together by drawing a line between them.

For working with hierarchical structure, users can drag writing
spaces inside other writing spaces to organise and reorganise the
text. Storyspace gives authors and readers multiple ways of viewing
and mapping the hypertext, to see both the hierarchical structure
and the links. The resulting hypertexts can be published on the web.
It is reasonably intuitive and there is a good manual in PDF format.

Toolbook

<http://home.click2learn.com/en/toolbook/>
An authoring tool intended for businesses designing courseware,
but used by innovative writers like M D Coverley who says of it,
'The minute I had created a page - text, sound, color, image – I was
enchanted with the process. By the end of the weekend, I had
mapped out the first version of *Califia*.' Users can build interactive
content-assessment objects, media players, navigation panels and
other interactive objects, many with predefined behaviours that
they can customise. There is a 30-day trial version, but the fully
fledged version runs into several hundred pounds.

Word Circuits Connection Muse

<http://www.wordcircuits.com/connect/> 115K download file
This is a set of software tools specifically for authors of web-based
hypertext poetry and fiction. Most hypertext tools available today for
the web are intended primarily for creating informational websites
where readers will usually browse (in the original sense of rather hap-
hazardly sampling some of the content), or seek out specific
information. Literature, on the other hand, demands a system designed
for whole-text reading – that is, one designed to accommodate readers who wish to consume an entire hypertext in a satisfying manner.

Writing courses in the UK

Acknowledgement to the National Association of Writers in Education (NAWE), *MsLexia* magazine and various colleagues for information sources. NAWE[67] has a database of courses, writers and links to major literature and education sites. Most, if not all, of the following will have further information about their courses available on the Internet.

Advances in Scriptwriting, Royal Academy of Dramatic Art
Applied Theatre MA, University of Manchester
Artists in Educational Settings, University of Derby
Artists in the Community, University of Central England
Certificate in HE (Creative Writing), accredited by the University of
    Liverpool
Creative & Media Writing BA, Middlesex University
Creative and Critical Writing, Ph.D. Cardiff University
Creative Arts Courses, The Indian King, Arts Centre
Creative Radio – Introduction, Thames University
Creative Theatre (New Writing), Central School of Speech and Drama
Creative Writing & Personal Development, University of Sussex
Creative Writing for TV Comedy, The Institute
Creative Writing MA, Bath Spa University
Creative Writing MA, Trinity College, Camarthen University
Creative Writing MA, Chichester University
Creative Writing MA, Plymouth University
Creative Writing, MA module, Warwick University
Creative Writing, Bath Spa University
Creative Writing, Bolton Institute
Creative Writing, University College, Chichester
Creative Writing, Lancaster University
Creative Writing, M.Phil, Cardiff
Creative Writing, Sheffield Hallam University
Creative Writing, the Arts & Education University of Sussex
Creative Writing, Trinity College
Creative Writing, University College Bretton Hall
Creative and Critical Writing, University of East Anglia
Creative Writing, Universities of Glasgow and Strathclyde
Creative Writing, University of Luton
Creative Writing and (choice of subjects) BA, University of North
    London
Creative Writing, University of Northumbria at Newcastle
Creative Writing, University of St Andrews

[67] <http://www.nawe.co.uk>

Creative Writing, University of Ulster
Creative Writing, Well-being, and Self-development Coastal Courses
Creative Writing: Poetry, The Poets' House
Creative Writing: Scriptwriting, University of East Anglia
Critical Creative Writing, Oxford Brookes University

Drama (Playwriting), University of Manchester
Drama and Theatre Arts, University of London, Goldsmiths College
Drama and Theatre Studies, University of Surrey, Roehampton
Drama, Theatre and Television Studies, King Alfred's College
Dramatic Writing, Rose Bruford College
Dramatic Writing, University of Sussex

English Literature and Creative Writing BA, University of Warwick

Film Making: Script to Screen, City University

Imaginative Writing, Liverpool John Moores University
Introduction to Screenwriting, Kensington and Chelsea College
Lifelines Open College of the Arts
Literature and the Internet, MPhil Birmingham University

Media and Performance, University of Salford
Modern Drama and Theatre Studies, University of North London

Narrative Writing MA, University of Derby
Novel Writing, University of Manchester

Performance Writing, Dartington College of Arts
Playwrights Workshop, City University
Playwriting, Greenhill College
Playwriting, Stages 1 and 2, The City Lit
Playwriting, The Method Studio
Playwriting, University of Birmingham
Poetry at the Abbey, Blue Nose Poetry
Poetry, University of Huddersfield
Prose Fiction, MA (Writing), Middlesex University
Reading Between the Lines, Open College of the Arts

Screen Thrillers, University of London, Goldsmiths College
Screenwriting – Film and TV, Richmond Adult and Community College
Screenwriting – Fiction, Leeds Metropolitan University
Screenwriting, Stages 1 and 2, The City Lit
Screenwriting, De Montfort University
Screenwriting, Liverpool John Moores University
Screenwriting, London College of Printing and Distributive Trades

Screenwriting, National Film and Television School
Screenwriting, Television & Radio Scriptwriting, University of Salford
Scriptwriting for Film and Television, Bournemouth University
Scriptwriting for Film and Television, University of Sussex
Scriptwriting for Film and Television, Epping Forest College
Scriptwriting For Film, Video and CD Rom, Central St Martin's College
    of Art and Design
Scriptwriting for Television, Stage and Radio, Thames University
Starting to Write, Open College of the Arts

Teaching and Practice of Creative Writing MA, Cardiff
Text and Performance Studies, University of London, King's College
The Short Short-story: Writing for Radio, The City Lit
The Teaching and Practice of Creative Writing, University of Wales,
    Cardiff
Theatre and Media Drama, University of Glamorgan
Theatre and Screen Writing, Mary Ward Centre
Theatre and Screen, Birkbeck College
Theatre Arts, University of London, Goldsmiths College
Theatre Practice, University of Exeter
Theatre Studies, City University
Theatre Studies, Liverpool John Moores University
Theatre Studies, Royal Holloway College, University of London
Theatre Studies, University of North London
trAce Online Writing School

Writers Lab, Raindance Film Workshop
Writing Advanced, Open College of the Arts
Writing and Creativity, University of Essex
Writing BA, Middlesex University
Writing Comedy, City University
Writing Courses, Fen Farm
Writing Courses, Ilkley Literature Festival
Writing Courses, Pecket Well College
Writing Courses, The Arvon Foundation (Devon)
Writing Courses, The Arvon Foundation (Inverness-shire)
Writing Courses, The Arvon Foundation (Yorkshire)
Writing Courses, The Hen House
Writing Courses, The Old School House
Writing Courses, The Poetry Business
Writing Courses, The Word Hoard
Writing Courses, Ty Newydd
Writing Courses, University of Leeds
Writing Courses, University of Sussex
Writing Courses, Westminster Adult Education Service
Writing Courses, Yorkshire Art Circus

Writing for Children MA, Winchester University
Writing for Children, King Alfred's College
Writing for the Stage, Arden Centre, City College Manchester
Writing for the Stage, Central School of Speech and Drama
Writing for the Theatre, London Academy of Playwriting
Writing for Theatre, Kensington and Chelsea College
Writing for TV, Radio and Theatre Workshop, Morley College
Writing MA, Middlesex University
Writing Situation Comedy, City University
Writing Situation Comedy, Morley College
Writing Studies, Edge Hill University College
Writing Television Drama, City University
Writing Two: Storylines, Open College of the Arts
Writing Two: the Experience of Poetry, Open College of the Arts
Writing, Edge Hill University College
Writing, Liverpool John Moores University
Writing, Nottingham Trent University
Writing, University of Glamorgan
Writing: Process and Practice, University of Wales, Aberystwyth

Experimental writers and word-artists

Mark Amerika: *Grammatron and How to be an Internet Artist*
<http://www.markamerika.com/>

Giselle Beiguelman: *The Book after the Book* and other works
<http://www.desvirtual.com/giselle>

John Cayley   <http://www.heelstone.com/meridian/cayley.html>

Bernard Cohen   <http://www.hermes.net.au/bernard/>

M D Coverley: *Fibonacci's Daughter* and *Califia* (and *The Personalisation of
Complexity* as Marjorie Coverley Luesebrink)
<http://www.cddc.vt.edu/journals/newriver/ 7/Fibonacci/choice.htm>
<http://califia.hispeed.com/califia.htm>
<http://trace.ntu.ac.uk/frame5/coverley/index.html>

Martha Conway: *Girl Birth Water Death* and other works
<http://ezone.org/ez/e2/articles/conway/>

Peter Finch poetry archive   <http://www.peterfinch.co.uk>

Caitlin Fisher: *These Waves of Girls*   <http://www.yorku.ca/caitlin/waves/>

Nick Fisher: *The Wheel of Fortune*   <http://www.bbc.co.uk/radio4/wheel/>

Diane Greco – experimental and critical works
<http://www.eastgate.com/people/Greco.html>

Caroline Guertin: *Queen Bees and the Hum of the Hive* (and other writings)
<http://beehive.temporalimage.com/archive/12arc.html>
<http://www.hypertextkitchen.com/WebHT. html>
<http://trace.ntu.ac.uk/traced/guertin/machine/>

Peter Howard's Poetry site   <http://www.hphoward.demon.co.uk/>

Shelley Jackson: *Patchwork Girl, My Body* and *The Ineradicable Stain*
<http://www.eastgate.com/catalog/PatchworkGirl.html>
<http://www.altx.com/thebody/>
<http://www.ineradicablestain.com/>

Michael Joyce: *Afternoon* and other works
<http://www.enarrative.org/>
<http://www.eastgate.com/catalog/Afternoon.html>

Talan Memmott: *Lexia to Perplexia* and *The Berth of V.Ness*
<http://www.altx.com/ebr/ebr11/11mem/>
<http://www.koreawebart.org/Talan_Memmott.html>

Mez (Mary-anne Breeze): *The Art of M[ez]ang.elle.ing* and *Cloh!neing God N Ange-Lz*
<http://netwurkerz.de/mez/datableed/complete/>
<http://www.javamuseum.org/st/artists/mez.htm>

Stuart Moulthrop: *Reagan Library* and other hypertexts
<http://iat.ubalt.edu/moulthrop/hypertexts/>

Lloyd Robson: *The Sense of City Road* <http://www.senseofcityrd.freeuk.com/>

Diane Reed Slattery: *Glide* <http://www.academy.rpi.edu/glide/>

Geoff Ryman: *253* <http://www.ryman-novel.com/>

Christy Sanford: *Web-specific Art and Writing* (*see*~~Water~~Water~~Water)
<http://fdt.net/~christys/>

Stephanie Strickland: *Ballad of Sand* and *Harry Soot*
<http://www.stephaniestrickland.com/>

Sue Thomas - writings <http://trace.ntu.ac.uk/suethomas/>

Helen Whitehead: *Web, Warp & Weft*
<http://trace.ntu.ac.uk/www/webwarpweft/index.htm>

Jody Zellen: *Ghost City* <http://www.ghostcity.com/>

Compendium sites

Two juke-box spread offered by the web artists Carolyn Guertin, Marjorie Luesebrink and Jennifer Ley, who produced two overviews with links to the work of 40 writers, artists and poets whom they judged were doing the best work in 2000:

The Progressive Dinner Party – showcasing women writers
  <http://califia.hispeed.com/RM/predinner.htm>

Jumping at the Diner – showcasing male writers
  <http://califia.hispeed.com/Jumpin/jukeframe2.htm>

Online communities and literary venues

Alt-X online publishing network   <http://www.altx.com/>

Digital Arts   <http:www.da2.org.uk>

Eastgate Systems – many interesting works of serious hypertext (offered for sale)   <http://www.eastgate.com/>

Electronic Poetry Centre   <http://wings.buffalo.edu/epc/>

e-Writers – community, competitions and advice – weekly online publishing newsletter   <http://e-writers.net>

e-Zone – literary site   <http://ezone.org>

Fiction Writer's Connection – provides help with novel-writing, and information on finding agents and editors and getting published; has mailing list of 3000+   <http://www.fictionwriters.com>

For writers – self-help; links and professional markets
  <http://www.forwriters.com>

HackWriters – UK-based free Internet magazine devoted to good writing, on any subject; no fees; forum of exchange   <http://www.hackwriters.com/>

Hyperizons – literary texts and criticism
  <http://www.duke.edu/~mshumate/hyperfic.html>

Journal of Digital Information – cinema and semiotics
  <http://jodi.ecs.soton.ac.uk/?vol=1&iss=7>

Kairos: A Journal for Teachers of Writing in Webbed Environments
<http://english.ttu.edu/kairos/>

Live Literature Network – add your name to a database of writers offering live events around the UK   <http://www.liveliterature.net/>

Metamorphiction – interactive fiction ideas book
<http://www.cobralingus.com/>

Mystic Ink – community areas for e-writers   <http://www.mystic-ink.com/>

National Association for Literature Development
<http://www.literaturedevelopment.com/development/>

New River Hypertext Journal – new works
<http://www.cddc.vt.edu/journals/newriver/>

Plexus – writings and visual works of several artists and writers
<http://www.plexus.org/>

Reactive Writing – exploring writing on the web
<http://www.reactivewriting.co.uk/>

Ring of Words – webring with 1000 other linked sites (some personal, some quirky), also has a chatroom
<http://www.poetrytodayonline.com/words/>

Slope – online eclectic yearnings in contemporary poetry and poetics
<http://www.slope.org/>

StudioNotes – service in entertainment industry to provide aspiring writers with the opportunity to develop and market their material; costly
<http://www.studionotes.com/>

trAce Online Writing Community – centre of experimental writing; also has courses   <http://trace.ntu.ac.uk >

UK artists (some writing installations)   <http://www.axisartists.org.uk>

Word Circuits – a community as well as a gallery of new fiction and poetry
<http://www.wordcircuits.com/>

Writernet – British community, mostly for writers working in theatre, television, radio, film, live art and performance poetry; a professional network.   <http://www.writernet.org.uk/>

Writers Net – a US-based forum for writers, editors, agents and publishers. Participants ex-change ideas about the writing life and the business of writing   <http://www.writers.net>

Writelink – UK resource site linking to paying markets, competitions, reference sites, software and so on   <http://www.writelink.co.uk/>

Writer's Website Discussion Board – mostly screenwriters (unmoderated)
<http://www.writerswebsite.com/ww/bbs>

The Writery Cafe – early community now looking its age
<http://web.missouri.edu/~writery/cafe.html>

Word Weave – writing tips, including character creation tutorial for beginner writers <http://www.welcome.to/wordweave

Writers on the Net – busy community offering online classes (paid for) <http://www.writers.com>

New media writing prizes

Among the criteria for the awards given below are:

- innovative use of electronic techniques and enhancements;
- literary quality, understood as being related to print and electronic traditions of fiction and poetry, respectively;
- quality and accessibility of interface design.

It is likely that awards such as these will grow over the next few years.

Bloggie Awards for the best web-logs (in 30 categories)
<http://www.fairvue.com/?feature=awards2002>
(note: change the year to the current one in the URL)

Dana Atchley Scholarship for Digital Story-telling
<http://ebookawards.org/>

Electronic Literature Awards – one for fiction and one for poetry
<http://www.eliterature.org/>

Eppie Awards for e-books (21 fiction and non-fiction categories)
<http://members.aol.com/seriouslywhacked/eppie_awards.htm>

Gutenberg-e – a prize competition for the best history dissertations in fields where the traditional monograph has now become endangered
<http://www.theaha.org/prizes/gutenberg/>

Independent e-Book Awards – for e-books and digital stories self- or independently published <http://www.digitalliteratureinstitute.org/>

Media Arts Plaza awards <http://plaza.bunka.go.jp/english/>

JavaMuseum online awards for innovative new media installations
<http://www.javamuseum.org/>

The trAce/Alt-X International Hypertext Competition
<http://trace.ntu.ac.uk/comp.cfm>

$100,000 annual prize for the best book published originally in electronic form; six smaller prizes in various categories. Search the Microsoft site for details <http://www.microsoft.com>

e-Publisher listing

Some of the main electronic publishers.

The e-publishers included in this table are all 'new' (i.e. not extensions of traditional houses). E-book manufacturers are not included; nor are the most blatant vanity presses (though it is sometimes hard to tell where subsidies end and self-publishing begins).

Authors thinking of taking a project to one of these publishers are advised to: enter into an initial dialogue by email, and judge the vibes by that; ask to be put in touch with one of their other authors; and, above all, check the contract in detail. If submission and contract details are not online, at least in broad outline, they may have something to hide (see also pp. 32–3).

Note: these details were correct at the time of going to press (June 2002) and may change.

Name, URL and location	Short description	Rights details	%*	Submission guidelines or costs
1stBooks Library www.1stbooks.com/ Bloomington, USA	E-book distributor (music, films and software too); offers books in PDF format; motley collection of stuff – Aesop's Fables is free while others sell for around $5.	Writers retain all rights, non-exclusive deal.	0–40	No guidelines – primarily a distributor. No cost to writer; titles produced in 2-3 months. Print on Demand takes longer.
The Author's Studio www.theauthorsstudio.org/ USA	Community of small presses owned and operated by commercial authors.	N/a	N/a	No details online.
Avid Press www.avidpress.com/ Michigan, USA	Seeking high-quality fiction novels to be published in e-book and/or print format; romance, mystery, gothic genre bias.	Contract online – publishers have exclusive electronic media rights.	30; 50 on sub-licence agreements.	Closes to submissions when over loaded. Email short synopsis, author blog and 1st chapter/prologue.
Artemis Press www.artemispress.com/ USA	Women's and lesbian fiction and non-fiction.	Contract online; exclusive rights requested.	40; 85 for subsidiary rights where publisher acts as agent.	Submission guidelines online, including word-count and manuscript formatting No fee.
Atlantic Bridge www.atlanticbridge.net/ Indianapolis, USA	Seeks sci-fi, horror, fantasy, paranormal; romance and mystery writers.	Non-exclusive contract; ask for electronic rights for one year. Sample contract online.	55	Submissions details online.
Back-in-Print (UK) www.backinprint.co.uk/ London, UK	Specialises in bringing out-of-prints titles back into print in small print-runs.	Sensible rights advice and FAQs.	N/a	N/a
Book4Publishing www.book4publishing.com/ Shropshire, UK	E-agent which showcases synopsis and first chapter and then auto-targets publishers and agents.	No info online regarding contractual agreement.	N/a	£39.95 fee for 12-month listing. No fee or royalties charged if work is taken up by a publisher.

Notes: * the percentage commission/royalty paid to the author; ** the share of advertising revenue paid to the author; all prices/fees correct at time of writing.

Name, URL and location	Short description	Rights details	%*	Submission guidelines or costs
BookLocker www.booklocker.com/ USA	E-book publisher-cum-bookstore, parent company of booklocker.com. Active promotion of its A-list. Uncertain benefits for others – relies on self-promotion as favours entrepreneurial authors. Two-tier system operates (e-book and POD), but there is an encouraging level of selectivity.	5-year exclusive reprint rights contract; tough on authors. Only requests non-exclusive rights.	E-book: 70 on books priced at $8.95 and over; 50 on those at under $8.95. POD: 35.	Detailed online guidelines. Work has to be polished (but there are templates and you can convert free) and over 100 pages. There's an Online Book Promotion Kit; there is also a $1.50 per month POD file hosting fee which is charged annually.
Book-on-Disk www.book-on-disc.com/ USA	Creates e-books in downloadable or disk format; pays royalties and appears to have been vetted by the American Authors Guild.	No contract online. Authors are free to list and sell their books elsewhere.	Is a royalty-paying e-publisher but no details online.	Submission guidelines online; closes when overloaded. Initial enquiries put on registration list until reopens. Work must be ready with cover art and editing complete.
Books on Line www.books-on-line.com	Opportunities to offer for books that have gone out of print, books by new authors, and reference books. Direct links to Amazon.com	Authors retain copyright but level of exclusivity is unclear. 2-year contracts (not online) for file transfers to downloads, diskettes, CDs, audio and multimedia sales Must allow them to sell book for minimum of 6 months.	10	No charges for books supplied in electronic form (don't specify formats); USA nominal fee of around $100 if they have to scan material, more to type and even more if have to 'read your handwriting'. Many pages are 2-3 years out of date.
BookZone www.bookzone.com/services/ epub.html Arizona,USA	Showcase service offering encrypted conversion to PDF, Rocket eBook, MSReader and Netlibrary amongst others. Offers Digital Rights Management protection. Also provides titles listings, e-book wholesale distribution, marketing, site development and other services.	Author-publisher retains control.	50 for POD and e-book service.	Multi-tiered pricing system; full details online. Submission guidelines online.
Boson Books www.cmonline.com/boson/ Raleigh, North Carolina, USA	Electronic book imprint of C&M Online Media Inc; eclectic list.	Seeks exclusive rights on a non-negotiable contract. Has a Writer's Program agreement.	N/a	N/a

Name, URL and location	Short description	Rights details	%*	Submission guidelines or costs
Centre House Press www.centrehousepress.co.uk/ Totnes, Devon, UK	Publishes excerpts of literary works of all types, where the respective authors intend subsequent full production in book form.	Details emailed on request; owner not seeking 'slush pile submissions'.	N/a	N/a
Crowsnest Books www.computercrowsnest.com/ London, UK	Science fiction, fantasy, horror, adventure, war, crime and thriller fiction novels; some non-fiction.	Full contract online; global sole and exclusive rights for 10 years.	40	Much the same as traditional book publishers; password area for accepted authors.
Diskus Publishing www.diskuspublishing.com/ Indiana, USA	Romantic fiction niche publisher. Books for several e-reader formats download for about £6.30 a book. Said to publish about 5% of submissions.	Sample contract online. Publisher asks for exclusive digital rights but author has some freedom of choice on which formats to allow.	40	Submission details available including word limit. Full manuscript required.
DLSIJ Press www.dlsijpress.com/ N/a	Fiction and non-fiction works by women authors, specialising in lesbian and gay material.	No contract online but some details are outlined in FAQ section. Grants electronic rights only.	45	Sensible submission arrangements and advice. Good FAQ section. Quirky design.
Domhan Books www.domhanbooks.com/ New York, USA	Multi-category genre listing for publication in a variety of formats.	Sample contract online.	Pays royalties but omits to specify percentage.	Submission guidelines online; approximately 1-2% acceptance rate.
eBooks.com www.ebooks.com USA	Internet Digital Bookstore; invites authors to let publisher or agent know about it as they don't deal direct with authors.	Authors should check rights deals with their publishers.	N/a	N/a
eBookWeb www.ebookweb.org/	Central source for news and information on all aspects of electronic publishing	Can submit pieces for column writing (unpaid) but not specifically an e-publisher for writers.	N/a	N/a
ENovel www.enovel.com/ Virginia, USA	Accepts books, stories, novellas and subscription stories.	Full downloadable agreement online; all e-rights throughout the universe for a period of 10 years.	50	Accepts manuscripts in either Microsoft Word or Word Perfect format on disk for a $25 upload fee. Otherwise free service offering 50% royalty on books, stories, novellas and subscriptions stories – beware the click copyright though; it's not necessary.

Name, URL and location	Short description	Rights details	%*	Submission guidelines or costs
Fatbrain www.fatbrain.com USA	Leading provider of books and information products to corporations. Also an 'Affiliate program' for authors, where you create a link to visit.Fatbrain through your own site and can collect up to 20% of any purchases made through each visit.	N/a	N/a	N/a
FictionWise www.fictionwise.com/ New Jersey, USA	Independent e-book publisher and distributor. Work must be previously published fiction by established authors. Cannot accept unsolicited material or work from new writers. Also distributes e-books from other quality e-publishers. Primarily interested in science fiction, fantasy, alternative history, horror, mystery, romance, action/adventure, mainstream literary, and humour categories.	Author must own electronic rights which FictionWise then purchases for a period of 5 years. Contract is sent out on acceptance of work. No contract details online. Royalty sales report available in realtime online. Affiliate Program service available with 15 % referral fees.	30	Must be established author with previously published works. Must supply minimum of 10 reprints. Submission guidelines online Minimum 5000 words.
Fiction Works typewww.fictionworks.com/ Oregon, USA	E-book and audio book opportunities.	Exclusive e-book rights sought with author retaining excerpt rights; publisher pays permissions and edits; moral rights in contract.	30	Very detailed guidelines including setting instructions; 40,000–150,000 words; sometimes closes to submissions.
Great Unpublished www.greatunpublished.com/ USA	Integrated community of writers, readers and professional editors. Self-publishing venue and bookstore; also provides a POD service.Useful and detailed info for authors. Operates a two-tiered system: basic kit includes formatting, cover art, e-book sales and on-demand paperback; special imprint program has more tailored benefits including author input on pricing, own cover specifications, choice of formatting and hard copy.	Detailed contract online for both programs. Non-exclusive, worldwide license in print and in all electronic media and all electronic formats in all languages.	30 on sales of books, 70 on sales of electronic files.	Comprehensive and detailed submission guidelines online. Basic minimum start-up fee \$199; Special Imprint Program \$299 – refundable to author if decide not to publish work. Any typographical/ editorial corrections in proofing process incur additional fee of \$100.

Name, URL and location	Short description	Rights details	%*	Submission guidelines or costs
Internet Book Company www.internetbookco.com/ Kentucky, USA, and Oxford, UK	E-bookstore with emphasis on history and travel genres, with a section on books for writers on writing, editing, publishing, etc. Open self-publishing environment with very little quality control – 'responsible free speech' ideology. Places warnings on controversial material. POD service available.	Contract available online. Exclusive electronic rights sought except audio and movie rights.	50	Submission advice and comprehensive FAQ. Submission fee $120 but does not guarantee publication; refundable if declined. Rate card also online for optional design, marketing and editorial services. Detailed description and advice on each service available.
iUniverse www.iuniverse.com/ Nebraska, USA	A multi-tiered service including professional feedback and showcasing service, and more traditional publishing options. Will offer stand alone e-book service in first quarter of 2002 (available as upgrade from POD service at the time of writing. Author-members of certain prestigious author associations get additional benefits, namely waiving of submission fees. Uses the Kinko Print On Demand system. Good Author Toolkit service with tips, advice and articles in e-zine format	Various contracts online; 3-year exclusive usages.	20–50	Full details on MSS preparation and requirements for OP submission; includes acceptable file formats. Publisher paginates and designs for the system – limits on final extent of the book. Author proof-reads. Fees range from $99 to $299 depending on service chosen.
Indipen www.indipen.com/ USA	Online literary/press agency and syndication service. Aims to help professional and semi-professional freelance writers promote their work to worldwide publications.	Sample contract online. Exclusive rights sought for duration of copyright and housing on website. Author can remove work from site which terminates agreement, except when work is sold to publication. Heavily weighted towards agent's legal protection. Read carefully.	Unclear on royalties; clause pertaining to works' 'consideration' less 15% Indipen commission – seems to require all-out sale	Submission details online. Sample work of 500-1500 words required to make suitability assessment.

Name, URL and location	Short description	Rights details	%*	Submission guidelines or costs
Infopost www.infopost.com/ New York, USA	Marketplace and portal for all things digital. Opportunities for authors to upload and sell books and articles directly.	General user agreement online, giving Buyer non-exclusive licence to use the content solely for own benefit. Site can't guarantee the accuracy, quality or legality of the content posted or sold, as doesn't pre-screen or censor content.	80	No fee to post material. Author responsible for uploading materials, setting selling price and providing description of material. Flexible approach to alterations and updating material. Can access reviews online and alter material or price accordingly. Similar look and feel to Amazon.
KnowBetterCom www.knowbetter.com/	Resource of information on the e-publishing scene, including latest info on technology, industry news, tips, advice and reviews. Useful overview and discussion forums.	N/a	N/a	N/a
Manuscript Depot www.manuscriptdepot.com/ Canada	Showcase for getting work to literary agents, publishers and film directors. Sample work in various categories is displayed and marketed. Some indication of track record – not enough.	No contract details.	40	Tips on how to get published. Costs $12-18 a month.
Mid West Book Review www.midwestbookreview.com Oregon, USA	Reviewing and resource portal giving priority consideration to small publishers, self-published authors, academic presses, and speciality publishers.	N/a	N/a	Submission guidelines online. Good links to writer and publisher resources.
My Publish www.mypublish.com Madison, USA	Sales resource for digital content. Provides commerce tools necessary to individuals and companies to become digital publishers. Anyone can publish, promote, sell or buy digital content online.	No contract details.	N/a	FAQ but no terms. Sparse details.

Name, URL and location	Short description	Rights details	%*	Submission guidelines or costs
netLibrary www.netlibrary.com Colorado, USA	E-book provider supporting missions and methods of libraries and librarians. Distributed through variety of channels including public, corporate, community and school libraries. Can only be read online; not compatible with other e-book readers or handheld at this time.	Only negotiates with publishers (including self-publishers?). Non-exclusive 3-year licence period.	N/a	N/a
Neighborhood Press www.neighborhoodpress.com/ Florida, USA	Small press publishing all types of fiction, from political mysteries to western historical romances. Offers three options for publishing: Neighborhood Press Published, Assisted Self Published and Self Published.	No online contract. NP ownership rights to be discussed at time of contract.	N/a	Accepts around 5% of submission. ASP program $400 initial set up fee; SP starts at $125. A little vague on contractual and royalty details.
Netspace Publishing www.netspace-publishing.co.uk/ Camarthen, Wales	Publishes electronic versions of texts not placed anywhere else. All books sold for £2.99.	Exclusive rights for 1 year.	30	Nothing online, but email requests give further information including contract details. Very sparse website.
New Concepts Publishing www.newconceptspublishing.com/ Georgia, USA	Specialises in romance and nostalgia – writers seeking publication; inexpensive for buyers; not obvious what the advantages to sellers are.	Exclusive electronic rights for a specified period, usually 3 years but sometimes less. Average contract is 2-5 years, negotiable with author Takes between 10-12 months to publish from contract signing.	$1 per disk or download sold directly through site. Retail royalties differ as contracts negotiable.	Traditional on-paper submission.
No Spine www.nospine.com/ London, UK	Self-publishing facilitator that takes 20% of whatever an author charges to cover e-commerce and web overheads. Quotes *Writers' & Artists' Yearbook* profusely. Track record unknown.	N/a	80	Submission guidelines online. No fee for submitting. Manuscripts must be full and single file. Formatting and proof-reading author's responsibility.

Name, URL and location	Short description	Rights details	%*	Submission guidelines or costs
Online Originals www.onlineoriginals.com/ UK	First online e-publisher established in 1996. One of several venues for new writers wanting to get published; aiming for upmarket products. Active promotional programme.	Nothing online, but generally seeks exclusive e-rights for the full term of copyright and right to be agent in all other media.	50	5 basic requirements: full book-length manuscript; available digitally in English or French language; original work; intelligently written; not previously published. Authors can commission reviews for £60 fee. Technical FAQ for submitting material. Neatly designed site.
Overdrive Systems www.overdrive.com/ Several US cities	How to publish with Microsoft Reader and other e-publishing solutions such as BookWorks; offers conversion services with full information on them all. Concentrates on commerce, enterprise, education and entertainment. Operates global marketplace and clearing house for digital content.	A partner in the new Open eBook Specification – no contract online, but clearly an authoritative set-up.	N/a	None. Confidence-making site. Has the gravitas of partnerships with several leading publishers. Gold Award for best e-book website through WHSmith.
Paperbackwriters www.paperbackwriters.co.uk/ Oxfordshire, UK	Showcase focusing exclusively on aspiring novelists in any genre looking for publisher.	Terms & Conditions online but no rights or royalties information.	N/a	Submission guidelines online. £30 to host a single work on-site for 12 months – website disclaims all liabilities; then 2% agents fee if author finds a publisher, in which case £30 is refunded.
Pulpless www.pulpless.com USA	Non-paper book publisher which claims to publish only established professional authors – opportunity to publish outside your usual category. Angled towards commercial works with a wide audience.	Non-negotiable 16-page contract. Seeks exclusive rights in paper and e-media form for on demand usages for the duration of the copyright.	6–25	Author pays prepress and other expenses. Tough. Looking for commercial projects with full manuscript. Heavily favours the computer-literate author. Detailed style sheet including technical specifications.
ReadMyWriting www.readmywriting.com/ Oxfordshire, UK	Print-On-Demand self-publishing resource for writers. Stated aim is to bring together authors, literary agents and publishers to enable the efficient publication of their work through the Internet.	Simple terms of business online; author retains all intellectual property rights.	100 minus £1 per copy for admin charges.	£350 service fee. Book illustrations are charged at £10 each. Work must be print-ready as no alterations are allowed once accepted. Cover art must be supplied by author. Comprehensive FAQ online.

Name, URL and location	Short description	Rights details	%*	Submission guidelines or costs
Replica Books www.replicabooks.com New Jersey, USA	Specialises in out-of-print books.	Contract and detailed pack mailed out to you: 7-year term with exclusive print rights.	Royalty-paying but does not specify %.	FAQ but no terms.
Roaming Reader www.roamingreader.com/	The classics delivered to your mobile phone. Possible opportunities for writers in the future.	N/a	N/a	N/a
Rosetta Books www.rosettabooks.com/ New York, USA	Sells and distributes books in various e-formats. No information for authors.	N/a	N/a	N/a
SellYourBooks www.sellyourbooks.co.uk/ Perth, Australia	Internet bookstore where established and new authors can upload and sell their work themselves.	No contractual information available.	N/a	£57 handling fee per upload for MSS formatting and showcasing books.
Small Press Center www.smallpress.org/ New York, USA	Non-profit institution for independent publishers. Useful articles and information for small publishers, including seminar and workshop details. A little out-of-date.	N/a	N/a	N/a
Tamarind Books www.tamarindbooks.co.uk/	Multi-cultural books for children. No info for authors.	N/a	N/a	N/a
Treeless Press www.treelesspress.com Berkeley, USA	E-book publisher of all genres; published through Barnes & Noble.	Contract downloadable online. Exclusive electronic rights.	20	No guidelines online but some info on formatting.
Unlimited Publishing www.unlimitedpublishing.com USA	Start here if you want to self-publish and bypass traditional publishers. A Print On Demand system for new and out-of-print titles. Co-publishes with authors and publishers, sharing 50/50 net profits.	No contract online.	50 if self-publishing.	Detailed submission guidelines online. Standard rate of $895 if MSS fulfils guidelines (using Word or similar). Gives details of its POD technology, clear costing details and sample materials. Must be minimum 100 pages.

Name, URL and location	Short description	Rights details	%*	Submission guidelines or costs
Virtual Volumes www.virtualvolumes.com/ USA	Search Engine for e-publishers online.	N/a	N/a	N/a
WordWrangler www.wordwrangler.com USA	Wild West publisher looking for a wide range of works.	Non-exclusive contract.	50–75	N/a
Write Online www.write-on-line.co.uk/ London, UK	E-texts and traditional print works for the academic market. Aims to secure hard-copy contracts.	No details online.	N/a	No guidelines online.
Writers Co-operative www.books-4u-online.com/ UK	Showcase for members of The Writer's Co-operative. Offers e-texts for £3 – author gets 'lion's share' (whatever that is). Also prints versions for £6.50.	N/a	50+	Enquiries by email only.
WritersServices.com www.writerservices.com/	Offers much-needed editorial services for writers as well as Information sheets by well-known writers pitched mainly at unpublished authors. Helps writers prepare for publication.	N/a	N/a	N/a
Xlibris www.xlibris.com/ Philadelphia, USA	Self-publishing centre; says it exists solely to serve and empower authors.	Detailed FAQ and terms of service online. Non-exclusive 'at will' agreement in operation. Authors retain all rights to their work.	10–50	Publication requirements for various services. Submission guidelines online. Fees $500 for Basic service; $900 for Professional; $1600 for Custom – details available for each service. Detailed and clear information.
Zipped Books www.zippedbooks.co.uk UK	Print on Demand, quasi-vanity press. Uses a specially developed format to read e-books on a browser.	Terms available online with sample contract.	25	£20 for a single copy of own book; any corrections incur a further £20.

And finally

Aladdin said: 'I beg of you, Princess, in God's name, before we speak of anything else, for your own sake and mine, tell me what has become of an old lamp I left on the cornice in the hall of four-and-twenty windows, when I went a-hunting.'

Whatever creative web writing can or cannot deliver, it should not be seen as a threat to more traditional literary forms. Digital works of art do not supersede analogue ones: they are something extra. If they have a future, it will be because they bring something fresh to our quest for making sense of the world. As this book has tried to show, we are not in a position to judge yet because the web is still too young a medium. We are looking at the working drawings, and not at the final edifice.

Computers and the Internet now surround us and it is inevitable that we should hunt out the artistic possibilities they provide. They force us to ask the question: 'Who are we in the digital age?' The answer must be that we're the same human beings as we always were. Computers haven't changed our ways of thinking, nor have they improved the quality of writing or of entertainment. There are limits to the ability of images on screens, or ideas marching across light-boxes or facts in databases to cater to our needs. We can push these limitations out to their edges, but not at the expense of swapping our exploration of the richness of the human spirit for expertise in computer technology.

Much of my reading (or viewing) in the course of writing this book has persuaded me that experimentalists are still at the stage of discovering what the technology can do. A small handful only have a vision, and understand what they are doing and why they are doing it. The 'Nouveaux Bloomsbury', as my quoted examples show, are deeply reflective. Others appear to feel that all's fair in the pursuit of what some are calling 'The Shock of the View'. That's a cliché; and we've been shocked too many times before. Why look back unless you are prepared to learn from what creative art-forms have worked in the past? It's all very well throwing out story, or meaning, or structure, or grammatical forms if you truly understand how to tell stories, or deliver meaning, or plan effectively, or write according to accepted syntax. Then you can experiment on the basis of what you know about your viewership. Then you can afford to play, or shock, or surprise. But I cannot escape the feeling that too much of what is on the web now is not art, but self-indulgence. I have a suspicion that there's a cult of being confusing just in order to be different. Confusion somehow fails to enthral.

For me, the trouble with subversion is that it must not be for subversion's sake. I recognise that questioning values is part of generating new literature, as I hope the explorations in the pages above have shown. The purpose of looking at the various literary experiments in this book is to see how visual word-play, randomising of texts, indulgence in nonsense and inconsequence, and mixing different media all exist within a tradition of departure from the mainstream of grammar and sequential narrative. Web writers appear to be going over the same ground again without asking what elements in these departures worked in their previous incarnations.

What is missing from much that I have seen is an exploration of human emotion, of characters growing through experience. Whether this fundamental lack is a temporary stasis while proponents play with the medium and learn what its assets and limitations are, time will tell. I believe there will be a return to an author–reader relationship in which the author posits a point of view and the reader assesses it. It has always been a two-way relationship; literature yielding different meanings at each re-reading. Artists are now trying to offer different readings at the same time. This is an exciting attempt and in consequence an exhilarating time for writers: those who find a way of combining the old accepted values with the new forms will succeed.

Of course, it is a two-way process. I have talked a great deal about how print creativity has fed into web creativity; conversely, new ideas about interactivity are feeding back into traditional literature. Ian McEwan's *Atonement*, from which I have quoted, has hypertextual elements to it that bring into question two versions of an event, and this device must derive consciously or subconsciously from what the web has brought to creative thinking. Similarly, the film *Sliding Doors*, with its two alternative stories based on a single node-point when a choice was made, brings hypertextual elements within a linear structure in ways that would not have worked some years ago. We are reading linear narratives differently now.

So one important reason for us to engage with web works – even if they are still hard to read and still lack a compulsive drive – is to enrich collective literature. We know that the web is compulsive; why should it not be possible to harness that to literature?

Bibliography

Bettley, James *The Art of the Book* London: V & A, 2001, ISBN 1-85177-333-9

Birkert, Sven *The Gutenberg Elegies* Canada: Ballantine Books, 1994, ISBN 0-449-91009-1

Chandler, Daniel *The Act of Writing* University of Wales, Aberystwyth, 1995, ISBN 0-903878-44-5

McKee, Robert *Story* London: Methuen, 1999, ISBN 0 413 71560 4

Murray, Janet H *Hamlet on the Holodeck: The Future of Narrative in Cyberspace* Cambridge, Mass: MIT Press, 1999, ISBN 0-262-63187-3

Lerner, Betsy *The Forest for the Trees: An Editor's Advice to Writers*, New York: Riverhead Books/Penguin Putnam, 2000, ISBN 1-57322-152-X

Johnson, Steven *Interface Culture*, San Francisco: HarperCollins, 1997, ISBN 0-06-251482-2

Webography

Chandler, Daniel 'Personal Home Pages and the Construction of Identities on the Web'. Available from:
<http://www.aber.ac.uk/media/Documents/short/webident.html>

Cramer, Florian: 'Digital Code and Literary Text'
<http://beehive.temporalimage.com/content_apps43/cramer/op.html>

Coover, Robert: 'Literary Hypertext: The Passing of the Golden Age'
<http://english.ttu.edu/kairos/5.2/reviews/rice/books.html>

Cramer, Florian 'Digital Code and Literary Text' in Beehive Hypermedia Literary Journal, 2001. Available from:
<http://beehive.temporalimage.com/content_apps43/cramer/oop.html>

Landow, George 'Hypertext: The Convergence of Contemporary Critical Theory and Technology' 1992. Available from:
<http://65.107.211.206/cpace/ht/jhup/contents.html>

Wittig, Rob: Observations From Here 'An E-Lit Writer Links to the Past' from Poets and Writers Online, 2001. Available from:
<http://www.pw.org/mag/wittig.htm>

Picot, Edward: Various writings on hypertext. Available from:
<http://www.edwardpicot.com/>

Sanford, Christy Sheffield: The Roots of Non-Linearity
<http://beehive.temporalimage.com/archive/31arc.html>

West, Misty: 'How to tell a story in 3-D space' 1997. Available from:
<http://www.vrmlsite.com/apr97/a.cgi/spot1.html>

Wiesner, Karen S. 'An Electronic Publishing Timeline' August 11, 2001. Available from: <http://12.108.175.91/ebookweb/stories/storyReader$328>

[All sites last accessed 10 June 2002]

Index